Warriors of Christendom

CHARLEMAGNE · EL CID · BARBAROSSA · RICHARD LIONHEART

JOHN MATTHEWS & BOB STEWART

Plates by JAMES FIELD

Firebird Books

First published in the UK 1988 by Firebird Books

Copyright © 1988 Firebird Books Ltd, P.O. Box 327, Poole, Dorset BH15 2RG
Text copyright © 1988 John Matthews *El Cid* and *Richard Lionheart*
R.J. Stewart *Charlemagne* and *Barbarossa*

Distributed in the United States by
Sterling Publishing Co, Inc
Two Park Avenue, New York, NY 10016

Distributed in Australia by
Capricorn Link (Australia) Pty Ltd
PO Box 665, Lane Cove, NSW 2066

British Library Cataloguing in Publication Data
Matthews, John, *1948*-
Warriors of Christendom: Charlemagne, El Cid, Barbarossa, Richard Lionheart.
(Heroes and warriors).
1. Europe – Warlords, 742–1200
I. Title II. Stewart, Bob III. Series
940.1'4

ISBN 1 85314 101 1

Series editor Stuart Booth
Designed by Kathryn S.A. Booth
Typeset by Inforum Limited, Portsmouth
Colour separations by Kingfisher Facsimile
Colour printed by Riverside Printing Co. (Reading) Ltd.
Printed and bound in Great Britain at The Bath Press.

Contents

Charlemagne

FOUNDER OF THE HOLY ROMAN EMPIRE

Charlemagne as depicted in a late sixteenth-century engraving of the Song of Roland in which he is described as the 'King with the grizzly beard'.

THE CAROLINGIAN EMPIRE

Frisia
Saxon March
SAXONY
Hamburg
Weser
Corvey
Paderborn
Rhine
Elbe
(Aachen)
AUSTRASIA
Amiens
Rouen
△Corbie
Cologne
Fulda△
BOHEMIANS
Noyon
Laon
Treves
Quimper
Brittany
St Denis
Soissons
Rheims
Frankfurt
Mainz
Worms
NEUSTRIA
Seine
Paris
△
Hautvilliers
Verdun
Nordgau
Brittanic March
Chalons
Lorraine
Moselle
ALEMANNIA
Swabia
Strasbourg
Ratisbon
Orleans
Sens
△Germigny-des-Pres
Loire
Auxerre
Luxeuil△
Danube
Bavaria
Kremsmunster△
Tours
Bourges
Besancon
Constance
St Gallen△
L.Constance
Inn
Augsburg
Salzburg
Poitiers
BURGUNDY
Chalon
L.Geneva
CARINTHIA
Pannonia
Saintes
Lyons
Rhone
L.Como
Friuli
Bordeaux
Garonne
AQUITAINE
Vienne
Valence
Milan
OMBARDY
Verona
March of Friuli
Aquileia
AVARS
Pavia
Cremona
Bobbio△
Genoa
Modena
Bologna
Ravenna
SERBS
GASCONY
Toulouse
Septimania
Avignon
Arles
PROVENCE
Pamplona
Navarre
Spanish March
Narbonne
Aix-en-Provence
Marseilles
Pisa
Gerona
Spoleto
Barcelona
Rome
ITALY
△ Monte Cassino

.... Extensions to the Empire made by 814 AD
—·—· Kingdom of the Franks in 771 AD when the death of Carloman united the territories under Charlemagne
△ Abbeys, priories and convents

6

Charles the Great

The achievements of Charlemagne – Charles the Great – were vast and complex. Perhaps the most telling aspect of his rule is that within a generation of his death, he was as much the subject of legend as of factual history. The power and skill of this one man built the great Frankish empire, and upon his death seemingly it died. But only in the territorial and political sense, for during his reign was born the important concept of the Holy Roman Empire. Initially, the political manoeuverings of Pope Leo III created the concept of the Empire, when he crowned Charles in Rome on Christmas Day of the year A.D. 800. Yet the new role of emperor was held in control by Charles who used it for his own ends, which were often of the highest order and extended far beyond mere materialism. Upon his death, the concept was to develop into one of papal supremacy over the emperor, a tense relationship which affected the future history of Europe.

In this study of Charlemagne, the emphasis is mainly upon two major aspects of his life: his military campaigns and his development of a unified European culture. Though the second aspect was short-lived, it remained as an ideal concept that inspired future kings and emperors; and the first has hardly been surpassed by any superior achievement to this day.

The history of those achievements is complex. Charlemagne fought and worked on several fronts at any one time; in the military, political and cultural senses. Thus, a simple linear record of his life and rule is impossible and cannot be pinned down as a simplistic historical account. Any narrative of his life develops along several parallel routes. A typical example is the pattern of revolt displayed by the conquered Saxons in what is now modern Germany. For much of his reign they persistently took advantage of Charles' absence in Italy or Spain to revolt against his rule. To give even a simple account of this sequence demands chapters that travel back and forth between the various territories that Charles conquered and ruled. Thus there is a pattern not only of territorial movement and campaigning, but of interaction through time, politics and dynastic struggles. In other words, much of the story weaves in and

Charlemagne and one of his sons, from the Leges Barborum, *a tenth-century copy of a Carolingnian manuscript.*

out, sometimes travelling back in time, sometimes forwards, in order to achieve a practical overview of the struggles and triumphs of Charlemagne.

Of particular importance to understanding Charles' rule is the need for a clear picture of the geography and political divisions of the huge territories over which he ruled. Without this, one cannot begin to grasp the size and complexity of Charles' achievements – such as the uncanny speed with which he could move troops across great distances. For example, he moved his army from Italy to Saxony to surprise tribes in revolt, a distance that is still great today with modern transport; but this the Franks traversed at speed with an army mainly on foot, with horse support and a massive baggage train.

Yet Charles' cultural achievements are as remarkable as his troop movements and campaigns: he was a builder, a political governor, a religious propagandist, and a reformer and patron of the liberal arts and sciences. It is inevitable that much will be omitted in this study but the bibliography lists several larger and more detailed works on specific aspects of Charles and his effect upon European history and culture.

8

The Franks

The Franks, over whom Charlemagne came to reign in the year 768, were originally a loose confederation of Germanic tribes. By the sixth century they had begun to force their way into Gaul (France and Belgium), and there they eventually settled. The modern name of France comes from the word *frank*, though the characteristics of the early Franks were very far removed indeed from those of the modern French peoples.

The invading Franks, wielding their famous *franciscas*, or short-handled throwing axes, fought on foot. They ousted the Gallic landowners who were the last remnants of the Roman Empire, conquered the Visigoths in the south of France, and fought other Germanic tribes, such as the Burgundians and the Alamanni, who were already settled there.

The great Frankish leader who unified the confederacy into a powerful entity was Clovis, first of the Merovingian kings. These rulers were replaced several centuries later by the House of St Arnulf, the family line of Charlemagne.

The Merovingian dynasty began as a vigorous force that firmly developed the Franks into a national entity, and made many conquests that extended Frankish territory. However, by the seventh century, the powerful blood of Clovis had been diluted considerably and King Sigibert III of the Merovings was a mere puppet under the control of his Mayor of the Palace. It was from these Mayors of the Palace – senior officers of the royal house – that Charlemagne's ancestors were eventually to become kings in their own right.

After further degeneration of the Merovings, and various attempts by ruthless Mayors to take full control of the kingdom, Pepin le Bref, the father of Charlemagne, was elected as King of the Franks in 752. Thus, within a period of about 300 years, the Franks had developed from a general confederacy of Germanic invaders with mere tribal links, into a fully-fledged kingdom. Furthermore, they had experienced the development and then degeneration of one major unifying royal line, the Merovings, and replaced this finally with a most vigorous governing family, the Arnulfings, who produced the great emperor Charlemagne.

System of Government

The Frankish system of rule was enlarged and refined under Charles, but was still very different from any system employed in modern history.

Frankish ornaments found in German grave; purse frame (above left) and (below) plaque, sword hilt and brooch.

Examples of early Frankish costumes.

There was no uniform code of law, and very little in the way of legal redress for common folk wronged by their superiors. Ultimately, all laws and decisions stemmed from the king, whose decree or word was absolute. Charles saw the wisdom of maintaining local traditions of justice in the varied regions of his great realm, and gave instructions that cases should be heard according to regional laws.

But authority was vested in the nobility, who held their power from the emperor. The line of power ran from emperor to king (Charles' sons) to sub-king, to duke, to count. The system of counties was essential to Frankish government, and a count could wield considerable power, particularly in far-flung regions.

To maintain some overall supervision of the nobility and the enforcement of royal decrees, Charles kept his court mobile, although his favourite and main palace was at Aachen. The term 'palace' originally referred to the gathering around the king, rather than an actual building. However, even with his extensive travels and campaigns, Charles could not maintain personal supervision of everything and so he appointed travelling supervisors or commissioners, known as *missi dominici*. This system was formalised in the year 802, although it had been operational in early forms during the preceding years of his reign.

Although such travelling overseers had been occasionally employed by earlier Frankish kings, Charles was the first ruler to define and formalise their role fully. The *missi* were both priests and laymen; they were appointed for a term of one year in specified countships and complaints against count or bishop were brought before them. In theory the system was efficient and just; in practice it was prone to the limitations of travel, seasons, and the possibility of corruption, which was inevitable in such an extended empire.

Man and Emperor

We have clear descriptions of Charles from his chroniclers and contemporaries; he is probably the first powerful figure to emerge from the Dark Ages as a completely documented ruler.

He was tall and stoutly built . . . his height just seven times the length of his own foot. His head was round, his eyes large and lively, his nose somewhat above the common size, his expression bright and cheerful. Whether he stood or sat his form was full of dignity; the good proportion and grace of his body prevented the observer from noticing that his neck was rather short and his person rather too fleshy. His tread was firm, his aspect manly; his voice was clear but rather high pitched for so splendid a body. His health was excellent; only for the last four years of his life did he suffer from intermittent fever. To the very last he consulted his own common sense rather than the orders of his doctors whom he detested because they advised him to give up the roast meats that he loved.

(from the chronicler Einhard)

Charles was described as temperate in his consumption of both food and drink (in an age and culture where gluttony and heavy drinking were often regularly practised by those who could afford it), and particularly careful when it came to alcohol. He is noted as drinking no more than three cups of wine or beer at a meal, and for punishing drunkenness among his followers.

He often said that religious fasts were bad for the health, and ate in moderation at all times. A typical meal would consist of perhaps four dishes, and his favourite hot roast on a spit, brought directly to his platter from the kitchen. Meals were enlivened by readings or poetry recited or chanted at Charles' command.

Charles was also an active man. He frequently rode and hunted, and enjoyed swimming, at which he excelled. Indeed, his capital city of Aachen (Aix la Chapelle) was partly chosen because of its hot springs, where Charles swam daily in the great bath.

He followed the Frankish manner of dress, hallowed by tradition, and did not wear exotic clothing, even at the height of his power. A typical costume would consist of linen strips wrapped around his feet and calves (stockings and similar wear had not yet been invented), high boots, a linen shirt and underwear, with a woollen overtunic and breeches. The tunic might have a silken decorative border, and in winter a fur coat of ermine would have been worn over the tunic. He also wore a typical bright blue cloak, and always carried a sword with a gilded hilt.

Charlemagne receiving the Oath of Fidelity and Homage from one of his barons in a cameo facsimile from the fourteenth-century Chroniques de Saint Denis.

11

On state occasions Charles dressed in a tunic and cloak embroidered with gold wire, fastened with gold buckles. He also wore a jewelled crown for such occasions, and a jewelled hilted sword. Yet in everyday dress he was noted for the simplicity of his clothing, and for not setting himself apart from his nobles in appearance.

He was very fond of ancient histories, stories and epics of earlier times and heroes. At this time much of the history was preserved in oral tradition, and there were long Frankish epic poems or cycles of ballads describing the deeds of his predecessors. Charles ordered these epics to be written out – although his son, Louis the Pious, unfortunately had them destroyed when he came to the throne, on account of the pagan content.

Charles also delighted in the works of Saint Augustine, and the *De Civitate Dei* was one of his favourite texts. He was able to read (in a time when many nobles were happily illiterate) and noted for his skill at reading aloud and singing to the harp. He also instructed those around him in these arts, and was far from being just a powerful military ruler. It is, indeed, this rounding and balance of his character and abilities that made Charles such a great ruler. Yet he seemed never quite at ease with his Christianity.

Church, Religion and Morality

For several centuries, Christianity had been the unifying political religion of the Franks. We find in Charles, however, an ambivalent attitude. He frequently attended church, and demanded strict attention and decorous behaviour from his court while at worship. We are told that he could pray in both Frankish and Latin, which was of course the official church language, although this reflects his facility with languages in general rather than any excess of devotion.

Yet he soon divorced his first wife, quite casually, to cement a treaty against his brother Carloman, and certainly paid little or no attention to orthodox Christian morality. On the death of his third wife, Charles lived with no less than three concubines who bore him numerous children. This pagan kingly behaviour (more reminiscent of ancient kingship rights than orthodox Christian behaviour) gave rise to criticism from the Church, but no one dared openly to accuse or chastise such a powerful ruler.

The relaxed morality of Charles himself extended to some, but not all, members of his large family. Two of his daughters lived 'in sin' without any comment from their father, but as soon as Louis the Pious inherited the crown, he banished these sisters to appease the Church and his own sensitive conscience.

Yet Charles was a mighty protector and sponsor of the Church, giving generously, building extensively, and installing clergy, churches and monasteries in his conquered territories. Little wonder that the savage

Saxons regarded Christianity as a Frankish method of suppression and control rather than a true religion in its own right. We might expect such a king to have been beatified upon his death (his ancestor had been St Arnulf) but Charles' indifference to Christian morality prevented this. Indeed, one Wettin of Reichnau, a visionary monk, claimed to have seen Charles in Purgatory, where the purifying flames burned away his lust in preparation for his entry into Heaven.

Charlemagne and his wife, from a ninth-century manuscript.

An impression of St Michael's Chapel at Fulda. This ninth-century, circular section is the only surviving part of the Abbey built by Charlemagne to enforce Christianity upon the pagan Saxons.

Frankish foot and horse warriors (opposite) armed with bows, spears and swords; from the ninth-century Golden Psalter in the monastery of St Gallen.

In retrospect, we can see Charles as a man of immense energy; we know from chronicles that he slept lightly and that he commenced state work very early in the morning, judging litigants in his private chamber. His astonishing capabilities in the arts and sciences, martial skills and campaigns, statemanship and administration, were simply reflected by his sexual life. Although the Church of the period lamented Charles' sexual vigour and lack of suppressive morality, to the modern imagination it seems remarkable that he could rule a vast empire and still have time to devote to three concubines. A weaker man might have become debauched (as many kings of that time certainly did) yet Charles clearly never allowed his vital energies to weaken his will.

On the negative side and however 'normal' for the period, we must remember that Charles was responsible for a number of massacres during his campaigns; in 782 at Verden, he ordered the slaughter of no less than 4,500 unarmed prisoners. Indeed he was notorious for his policy of 'baptism or death' in respect of the Saxons.

Crowning Victories

On the death of Pepin le Bref, his sons Charles and Carloman immediately had themselves proclaimed as kings by their supporting nobles, and were anointed by their respective bishops. Thus when Charles gained his first crown on 9th October 768, he was far from sole ruler or great emperor. This division of the realm was according to Frankish custom, under which sons shared inheritance of their father's dominions. It had often proven to be a disastrous, or at best weakening, influence upon the stability of the realm, as the inevitable feuds between factions arose from such divisions.

But Pepin had perhaps left his first-born, Charles, superior in power to Carloman, though they ruled jointly from 768 to 772. By the simple expedient of giving Charles control of the military elements of his kingdom, Pepin may have ensured that his elder son would retain greater control. Charles ruled all the Frankish territories which provided the fighting men: from the Main to the Channel, the Austrasian and Neustrian warriors were under his command. He also inherited the western part of Aquitaine, which had been added to the kingdom by conquest in 767, not long before his father's death.

Carloman inherited rulership of Burgundy, Suabian territories on both sides of the Upper Rhine, and the Mediterranean coast from the border of Spain to the Maritime Alps; he also acquired the eastern part of Aquitaine. Thus although his territories were extensive and almost equal to those of his elder brother, the military might and command of the famous Frankish warriors remained mainly with Charles. It was therefore Charles who could dictate policy and law in most respects.

This allocation of power by Pepin was probably based upon his recognition of a feud between Charles and Carloman who, of course, remained unfriendly towards one another after their respective crownings and inheritances. Although Charles was the eldest son, he had been born while his father was still Mayor of the Palace. Carloman, however, had been born after Pepin had been crowned king in his own right and so considered that he held a superior claim to kingship.

As it turned out, the joint reign was short, no more than three years, during which time the feuding brothers were kept in check by the influence of their mother Bertha. Then before an outright war between Charles and Carloman could erupt, the younger brother died, leaving the way open for the development of one of the greatest European emperors in history – but not before earlier triumphs.

Reconquests of Aquitaine 769

As soon as Pepin le Bref was dead, Aquitaine revolted, presumably hoping to take advantage of the disagreement between the old king's heirs and re-establish independence. The ruling Duke Waifer had been

Overseen by evangelist monks, Charlemagne's conquering Franks meet fierce resistance from Saxon tribesmen. The superior might of the Frankish army was often hard pressed in the Saxon wilderness.

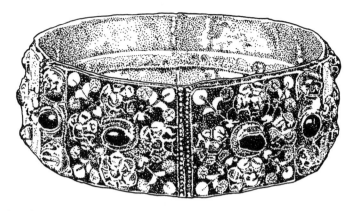

killed in the war with Pepin, but his father, Hunold, came out of retirement in a monastery to lead the revolt. Support for the aged warrior extended as far north as Angouleme and seemed to present a serious threat to Frankish rule in Aquitaine.

Charles, now commander of the military strength of the kingdom, marched with a large force to subdue Hunold and his supporters. He invited his brother Carloman to join in the campaign, but they argued immediately, and Carloman returned to Burgundy, leaving Charles to continue alone in the reconquest of Aquitaine.

As a result of his leadership, the Frankish army fought through to Bordeaux and built a huge fortified camp at Fronsac. This camp was so strong that it remained as a major fortress for the Garonne region for centuries to follow. The aged Duke Hunold was defeated, and fled to take refuge with Lupus, Duke of the Gascons. But Lupus shrewdly submitted to Charles, gave up the offending Aquitaine leader, and was granted peace. Charles returned in great triumph, indisputable King of Aquitaine. Hunold was not executed, as we might expect, but returned to the obscurity of his monastic life. As a final stroke, Charles divided Aquitaine into countships, the customary Frankish mode of government, placing the command with men from north of the river Loire, who were entirely his own.

After the reconquest of Aquitaine, Bertha persuaded Charles towards a reconciliation with his brother. But Charles was already demonstrating his statesmanship, making treaties with various rulers whose territories bordered upon those of Carloman. These included Tassilo, Duke of Bavaria, and Desiderius, King of Lombardy. In these moves Charles was displaying the combination of martial skill, courage, and shrewd politics that were to become such a feature of his rapid growth from king into emperor.

To cement the alliance with Lombardy, Charles married Desiderata, the daughter of Desiderius. This political marriage was very unpopular with Pope Stephen III, especially as the papacy had encouraged the Frankish kings to weaken the power of the Lombards, whose territories

The Iron Crown of Lombardy worn by Charles after his conquest of Desiderius. It was said to have been made from a nail of the True Cross, with ornamentation of gold, enamel and jewels.

Saracen ambassadors bring Charlemagne a white elephant, complete with exotic trappings. Becoming very attached to this curious animal, he took it on extensive travels until its death.

bordered upon its own. Charles was requested by Stephen 'not to mix the famous Frankish blood with the perfidious foul leprous Lombard stock – a truly diabolical coupling which no true man could call a marriage . . .'

But Charles was securing his own interests rather than those of the Pope, and proceeded with the marriage despite every threat and protest. After all, Charles never seemed to have held much regard for Christian morality and marriage laws, and certainly was not likely to let papal complaints and rhetoric alter his decisions. Stephen, however, as soon as the marriage with Desiderata was consummated, abandoned all his objections to the 'foul leprous Lombards' and entered into a treaty with Desiderius. Presumably the thought of a combined Frankish and Lombard opposition was too disturbing to bear.

After one year Charles suddenly divorced Desiderata on the grounds that she was barren and weak. He immediately married a Suabian noblewoman called Hildegarde, and so gained a new wife and the unrelenting hatred and opposition of his ex father-in-law.

The Death of Carloman

In 771 it seemed likely that Desiderius would join forces with Carloman against Charles, but in December of that year, the younger Frankish king died. Although Carloman had an infant son, the nobles and bishops of Alamannia and Burgundy immediately travelled to Corbeny-sur-Aisne to do homage to Charles. Suddenly he was ruler of all the Frankish realms.

Opposition to Charles was now centered in Lombardy at the court of Desiderius. Carloman's widow, child, and a small band of supporters were welcomed by the Lombards, who pressed the child's claim to a share of the Frankish kingdom. Despite this counter-claim, Charles now ruled an extensive area: all lands from the Main to the Bay of Biscay, and from the mouth of the Rhone to the mouth of the Rhine, were under his sole dominion. It was a realm controlled by the disciplined military might of the Franks.

Frankish Warfare

There are conflicting theories regarding the methods of combat used by the Franks at the time of Charlemagne. Although Norman horsemen used stirrups, a major invention and development in terms of medieval warfare, it is not certain if the warriors of Charlemagne used them to any great extent. A Frankish stirrup has been discovered by archaeologists, but contemporary records do not confirm that horse charges and similar tactics were widely used.

The soldiers of Charlemagne.

The early Franks fought on foot, using spears and single-handed axes, usually with the protection of a shield wall. But by the time of Charlemagne the majority of warriors were on horseback, though it is not clear if they actually *fought* from horseback or if they used the horses simply as rapid transport for traditional Frankish foot soldiers. It is probable that this was a transitional period, in which cavalry techniques and the use of stirrups were being developed, while the earlier form of the armed group and shield wall was still extensively used.

Weaponry and Equipment

Perhaps the most famous weapon of the Franks was the sword: Frankish swords were in great demand across Europe for their balance and temper, and a number of restrictions were issued by Charlemagne controlling their export. The fact that these were generally long swords tends to confirm the use of cavalry. On horseback the long reach of the swordsman is supported by his horse, enabling him to use with great effect a weapon that might be cumbersome on foot.

Ornate sword, reputedly Charlemagne's. Frankish swords were the best in Europe; strict legislation was enforced by Charlemagne to prevent exports beyond his realm.

Infantry carried short swords – the scramasax of Germanic origin. This had a single edge and a thick, heavy blade which could also be used as a bludgeon (the 'flesh cutter' and the 'bone breaker'). Each foot soldier also carried a bow, twelve arrows and a spare bowstring as standard equipment. Finally, they also carried spears. The implication is that the Frankish foot soldier was skilled in all round weaponry, able to fight at a distance and at close quarters. They did not wear much in the way of body protection or helmets (early Frankish shield bosses were at first classified as helmets by early archaeologists).

The horse soldier, however, with his longer sword, wore leather armour in the form of a jerkin or jacket sewn with iron plates reaching to his thighs. He also wore a helmet, and carried the traditional scramasax as a second sword, as well as a spear with a large crosspiece behind the blade, and a round shield.

The typical crosspiece of the Frankish spear implies the use of the weapon from horseback. Without the crosspiece the considerable force of a horse charge would mean that the weapon might be impossible to reclaim or be pulled from the rider's control after striking. From the equipment, we can see that the Frankish horse soldier was in the earliest stages of development into the armed and armoured knight of later centuries.

The Army

The remarkable achievements of Charlemagne are further emphasized by the fact that he did not have a standing or regular army at any time. All Frankish freemen were required to serve in campaigns when summoned, unpaid and providing their own equipment. We have evidence that booty was divided among the troops as a fairly regular method of

Typical Frankish arms and shields, including the francisca *or war axe.*

reward; during the conquest of the Avars, there was even sufficient loot to send gifts to distant Mercia in England. The major divisions went to the nobility, of course, but a Frankish soldier had to fight on command, in the hope that a successful battle or campaign would realise some spoil for himself.

The growing use of cavalry, however, tended to exclude the poorer freemen from fighting in full equipment, and only those with four hides or more of land were required to equip themselves. Mustering was administered by the counts, who were frequently accused of bribery and coercion in the tally of the muster. If anyone failed to attend the muster, heavy fines and punishments could be imposed.

It was the military custom of the Franks to gather the army in spring, and to remain active for three to six months. Under severe campaigning requirements, soldiers could miss both spring planting and autumn harvest, but all campaigning ceased for winter although sieges were sometimes maintained through the winter months by means of entrenched camps and containing earthworks. In many cases the army was mustered as late as May, to allow snow to recede from remote areas, such as the much used Alpine passes.

Soliders were required to bring with them three months' supply of provisions, arms, armour and tools for entrenching and other tasks. Charlemagne was particularly well organised in terms of military mobility and supplies; advance planning was carefully worked out and supplies were often requisitioned in the season before the actual campaign. Herds of cattle and extensive baggage trains followed the troops; the famous romantic exploits of the hero Roland are derived from a historic defence of one such train.

Plundering *en route* was forbidden, probably because it reduced the speed of the army rather than for any ethical reasons. During the Saxon rebellions, however, general looting was allowed as form of punishment for the rebels and as part of a considered plan of devastation. The reward of the soldier, as we have mentioned, was booty from fortified locations taken in battle, and the right to strip the dead of the opposing forces on the battlefield.

Tactics

The planning which made Charlemagne such a successful campaigner was not limited to the organisation of the army's stomach; he employed extensive advance information, usually gathered and considered in the year before each campaign. Every detail of the proposed territory for conquest was examined: population, geography, methods of war, domestic and agricultural patterns of life. This disciplined approach was unusual for the time, and indeed, many later medieval wars were conducted in a far more haphazard manner.

Although an energetic and able warrior, Charlemagne tended to direct

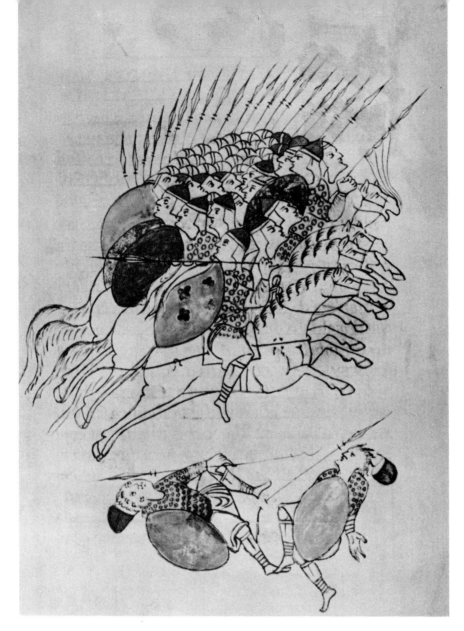

battles rather than fight in person. Once again we find that his methods of command were innovative and successful. His favourite tactic was to divide his forces into two armies, one under himself or a son, and the other under a powerful noble with experience of battle. This two-fold method of invasion, combined with the almost legendary speed of the Frankish forces, tended to keep Charlemagne's opponents confused and uncertain, and when the two forces of the Frankish army reunited, it was usually to deliver a crushing attack upon the targeted opposition.

There is no firm body of evidence of any sophisticated tactics; the foot soldiers were divided into groups who supported the horse soldiers and some men, as we have suggested, rode into battle but fought on foot. The cavalry technique would have been the single mass charge carrying maximum force, with following attacks from foot soldiers. The foot

Armed Frankish horsemen from the Book of Maccabees, *a tenth-century Swiss manuscript from St Gallen. The stylised formation suggests a charging battle tactic. Round shields, chain mail and simple conical helmets are clearly visible.*

21

were also responsible for entrenchments and for engineering works associated with sieges. Archery seems to have been a minor technique, for men armed with swords and spears and carrying only twelve arrows could hardly be termed 'archers' in the later medieval sense of a specialised separate force of skilled bowmen used as a collective weapon in their right.

First Campaigns

Among the many achievements of Charles, the most obvious is the extent of his military conquests. During his reign he added vast territories to the Frankish kingdom that he had inherited; Lombardy (the traditional enemy of both Franks and papacy), parts of Spain, all of Saxony over a prolonged period of campaigning, and Slavonic regions of the Drave and Elbe.

There is no doubt whatsoever that this expansionism was a deliberate and carefully controlled policy; Charles did not fight defensive or reluctant wars. He greatly amplified the Frankish role, established by his predecessors Charles Martel and Pepin le Bref, as defender of Christianity allied primarily (but not always harmoniously) with the Roman pope rather than the Christian hierarchs and rulers of the Eastern Roman Empire based in Constantinople.

This politico-religious stance originated in the necessary defence of Western Europe from the Slavs, Saxons and Saracens, three pagan and savage races who continually sought to invade. But Charles was not merely a defender, and while his ancestors had often been weakened through internal dissent among the Frankish nobility, he had total command and a clear field of action based upon considerable personal and state resources. Thus he actively sought to crush the Slavs and Saxons, and forcibly render them Christian, just as his grandfather Charles Martel (who died in 741) had converted the Frisians and Thuringians.

It was not possible, however, to 'convert' the Saracens; they had a policy of religious expansionism too – seeking to convert all unbelievers to Islam at the point of the sword. Charles sought to expel and chastise the Saracens, keeping them out of his southern territories and securing border areas where they might encroach.

The Lombards were a different matter, for they were a Christian state in Italy. Charles' father, Pepin le Bref, had allied himself with the papacy against Lombardy, but Charles eventually destroyed the Lombards and took the Iron Crown for himself. While this may seem a consolidation of his European realm and role, Charles could not have foreseen that he was

Bronze casting of Thor, the thunder god, who was worshipped extensively in northern Europe at the time of Charlemagne's enforced military evangelism.

to strengthen the future power of the papacy far more than that of his own lineage. When Charles received the (initially) doubtful title of emperor from Pope Leo III on Christmas Day, 800, he set the scene for later claims that the Pope had the power to install, or to depose, the Emperor.

Spearmen from the ninth-century Apocalypse de Saint Amand. The spears have the typical cross-piece of Frankish weapons.

Boundaries of the Realm

At the time of Carloman's death and Charles' succession as sole ruler, the Frankish realm was extensive, but by no means comparable to that later established by Charles himself.

In Germany the northern border was held by the Frisians, and the southern border by the Bavarians. These tribes had been conquered by the Franks and forced into Christianity, but they retained their own kingship or leaders, and were not tightly bound to the Frankish throne in terms of direct government.

To the east of Frisia were the pagan Saxons, a diffuse and essentially nomadic conglomeration of tribes. Despite 300 years of conflict, the Merovingian kings and their Mayors (who eventually became the Frankish kings in their own right) had found it impossible to subdue the Saxons on any permanent basis. Beyond the Saxons, further east, were the Slavonic tribes of the Sorbs, Abotrites and Wiltzes, also pagan and virtually unknown to the Franks.

To the east of Bavaria were other Slavonic tribes, Czechs, Moravians and Carentanians. Beyond these lay the large realms of the Avars, who were Tartar tribes unified under a ruler known as the Chagan.

Soldier's ornamental helmet from a Frankish grave.

23

Between Frisia in the north and Bavaria in the south, the frontier inherited by Charles was held by the Thuringians, who were ruled by Frankish counts. This conquered territory was totally under Charles' control and bordered on the territories of the unconquered Slavonic Sorbs. We will find this system of countships or counties recurring as a basis of Frankish government when we examine the campaigns against the Saxons in detail. The term 'county' for an administrative area is still found in Europe and America today.

To the south-east lay the great mountain chain of the Alps, acting as a barrier (soon to be overcome by Charles) between the Franks and the kingdom of Lombardy. The south-west was bounded by the Pyrenees, beyond which lay the Saracen territories of Spain. At the time of Charles taking his crown, the Saracens were ruled by Abd ar-Rahman the Ommeyad, who had declared his own state independent of the main Abbaside caliphate in 755.

The territories described above were all to feel the military might of the Franks under the remarkable leadership of Charles the Great.

Invasion of Lombardy

King Desiderius, as we have seen, received Carloman's widow Gerberga and her son and supported their claim to the Frankish crown. Lombardy was the first territory to be invaded by Charles, but the Lombard support of the Carloman faction was not the official or even the major reason for the campaign.

The new pope, Hadrian I, repudiated the Lombard alliance made by his predecessor, and demanded territories from Desiderius. He claimed that Ferrara and Faenza had been promised to papal authority in 757 as part of the Exarchate of Ravenna before Desiderius became king and while he was still struggling for the crown with his rival King Ratchis. When this papal claim was made, Charles was busy annexing the territories of the newly deceased Carloman, and seemed unlikely to offer the traditional Frankish support to the pope against the Lombards, based on agreements made by his father Pepin le Bref.

Desiderius responded to the Pope by raising an army and seizing Sinigaglia and Urbino, hitherto papal cities. He then mobilised his full military potential and marched against Rome. Hadrian had already fortified the city and brought in heavy garrisons for defence; he now sent to Charles invoking the agreement between the Franks and the papacy. The Frankish king was expected to enforce the treaty imposed upon the Lombards by his father Pepin, and drive them back to their own territories.

Desiderius, perhaps surprised by this indication that Charles was not so occupied after all, drew back to Viterbo. He then sent a counter-embassy to Charles (in the autumn of 772), explaining that he was not

Armed Frankish horsemen (opposite) as shown in the Golden Psalter. The riders use stirrups and large, supporting saddles, so may be a cavalry unit. They have mail tunics and basic helmets, whilst their banner is a typical 'dragon' or tubular device carried on a long shaft.

ETSYRIAM SOBAL · ET CONVERTIT
IOAB · ET PERCVSSIT EDOM INVAL
LE SALINARVM · XII MILIA ·

unlawfully retaining those lands claimed by the Pope on behalf of the Exarchate of Ravenna, as the claim was false.

First Saxon Campaign

Charles, meanwhile, had commenced his first campaign to subdue the Saxons, a task which was not concluded for over 20 years. In the summer of 772 he led an army into middle Saxony, and took hostages from the Engrians. He then destroyed the *Irminsul*, a sacred temple or tree grove worshipped by all Saxony. This religious sanctuary stood near Paderborn, and was a type of national spiritual or magical centre for the widely scattered and nomadic Saxon tribes. Tree worship of this sort was a feature of pagan Germanic, Norse and early Celtic culture, and is still found in myth, legend and folklore in many variant forms. The *Irminsul* was laden with rich sacrificial offerings of wealth, which were plundered by the Franks.

When Charles returned to Austrasia in the autumn, he met the ambassadors of both Hadrian I and Desiderius at Thionville. He supported the Pope, of course, and sent his own embassy to the Lombards demanding that Desiderius remove his forces from the occupied papal cities, and comply further with the Pope's original demands for Ferrara and Faenza. Desiderius refused to obey or accommodate in any way.

By this time winter had arrived, when campaigning usually ceased. We need to remember that, unlike modern warfare, medieval campaigns were seasonal. This seasonal element in warfare persisted as late as the nineteenth century, but in the period of Charles it was often impossible to wage war in the winter, both because of the weather, and because of the basic necessity to harvest crops in autumn for survival of the people. Thus even a standing army (not known in the modern sense at this time) took time off in the winter. Charles' command was based upon support of his nobles, tributary rulers, and their own dependent households and levies; this formidable fighting force was reconvened in the spring of 773 to invade Lombardy.

Return to Lombardy

They marched from Geneva, Charles leading one army over Mont Cenis, while his uncle Bernard led another through the Great St Bernard Pass. The access to Lombardy had already been fortified by Desiderius, with defensive positions in the Alpine gorges at Ivrea and Susa. But a band of Franks climbed over the mountains at Susa and outflanked the Lombards, forcing Desiderius to fall back upon Pavia.

Charles followed his advance band rapidly, and laid siege to Pavia for several months. During this prolonged siege, Desiderius' son Adelchis raised a second Lombard force and took position before Verona. Leaving the blockade of Pavia to a smaller force, Charles marched directly against Lombard the heir Adelchis, taking Verona, Brescia and Bergamo. The unfortunate Lombard prince fled to Constantinople, where he sought help from the Eastern Emperor Constantine Copronymus.

During the prolonged siege of Pavia, with no sign of capitulation from King Desiderius, Charles spent the spring of 774 in Rome. He held meetings there with Hadrian I, and the two leaders, spiritual and temporal, each seeking political self advantage from the other, came to certain understandings.

Charles arrived in Rome, perhaps intentionally, during Holy Week, and celebrated the Easter festivities there in great ostentation and style. His discussions with the Pope led to Charles' confirmation of papal rights over the Exarchate of Ravenna, from Ferrara and Commachio in the north, to Osimo in the south. This grant included those territories or cities disputed between Lombardy and the pope, and basically reaffirmed arrangements made between Charles' father, Pepin le Bref, and Rome. Such a confirmation was to be of great propaganda value to the papacy in addition to its immediate political and financial value; Charles had confirmed that a friendly relationship existed between the great kingdom of the Franks and Rome, and that a pope could make demands upon the Frankish king in full expectation of support and response – perhaps even of obedience.

Submission of Lombardy

By the summer of 774 Pavia was in a state of famine from the long siege, and Desiderius agreed to submit and open the gates on the condition that his life and those of his men would be spared. The Lombard king was exiled to Neustria, and later became a monk in the Abbey of Corbey where he died in his old age. The Lombard royal hoard was divided, as was often the custom, as loot for the Frankish army. Regular pay was not known in those days, and booty was the usual form of reward at the successful conclusion of a campaign.

Prince Adelchis had become a client or patrician at the court of Constantinople; this left Charles free to have himself proclaimed as king in Italy. He ordered all the Lombard dukes to pay homage to him at Pavia, and from that time onwards was known as 'King of the Franks and Lombards, Roman Patrician'. Charles did not make extensive changes in the Lombard government, and retained many of the governors and administrators who had originally served under Desiderius. Some Italian cities were given to Frankish counts in the usual manner, and a garrison was left at Pavia. This moderate policy ensured that Italy would not be a perpetual hotbed of revolt and dissension.

But Arichis of Benevento, son-in-law to Desiderius, refused to do homage to Charles, and in 776 Benevento, Fruili and Spoleto attempted to restore the exiled prince Adelchis. Charles responded immediately, and on this second expedition into Italy, killed the Duke of Fruili in battle. Spoleto was forced to do homage, but Arichis maintained his

Frankish warrior from the time of Charlemagne.

independence in the south until 787 when Charles again entered Italy in person, besieged Salerno, and finally subdued the obstinate duke.

Conquests of Saxony

While Charles was busy fighting the Lombards and making his terms of future agreement with the Pope, the Saxons revolted against Frankish rule and by 775 we find Charles once again marching his armies into Saxony. This was an action that he was to repeat many times before any true subjugation of the Saxons was achieved.

Saxony was divided into four large regions. Closest to the Frankish frontier was Westphalia, whose tribes lived on the Lippe and Ems, and in the region about the Teutoburger Wald. Further east were the Engrians (who had been temporarily subdued in the summer of 772) whose territory included the valley of the Weser, from its mouth to the borders of Hesse. Further east again was Eastphalia, on the Aller, Elbe and Ocker. The Elbe divided the Eastphalians from the Slavonic Abotrites. The fourth Saxon region was that of the Nordalbingians in Holstein, beyond the Elbe, bordering upon Denmark. These were the most savage and primitive of a generally savage race.

Saxony was a wild land in its natural state of heath, marshes and woods. The main hills were in the south, where Saxony included the outriders of the Hartz mountains. There were no towns or large settlements, and very little in the way of static fortification or any points of specific location, though entrenched or mound camps were known. This made conquest almost impossible, as there was nothing to conquer in the customary sense of European or Asiatic warfare.

When the Frankish armies entered Saxony, the Saxons usually hid in the endless forests or untracked marshlands; there they simply waited until the Franks had marched through, and emerged either to harry from behind or continue their nomadic life in another area. There were no roads of any sort, and rapid pursuit of tribal groups was out of the question.

The only viable tactic seemed to be to surround the tribal hosts, forcing them to give hostages and cattle in exchange for leniency. Once the Franks had departed, however, the tribes simply proceeded with revolt and did their best to destroy any remaining Frankish outposts or sympathisers.

When Charles cut down the sacred tree *Irminsul*, he was destroying the one central element of Saxony that all tribes seemed to look to and respect. This one act earned him unfailing hatred and opposition. However Charles saw his conquest of Saxony, it must have seemed to

The Enger Reliquary showing the figures of Christ and the Virgin accompanied by angels and apostles. This gold-covered oak cask was given by Charles to the Saxon chieftain Wittikind as a gift when he finally surrendered and accepted baptism in the year 785.

the Saxons to be a religious war, for they had no firm concepts of centralised government, only tribal nomadic territories, and certainly no need for the town, city and county based Frankish system. The imposition of Christianity upon the greater part of Saxony took Charles until the very end of his long life.

To gain the upper hand Charles had to repeatedly invade and conquer the four Saxon regions; he used drastic techniques of extermination and punishment; he transplanted entire tribes forcibly to weaken any sense of identity and revolution; he built towns, churches and castles wherever possible, and supported large numbers of Christian missionaries to the pagans by force of arms.

In 775 Charles began by invading Westphalia, dispersing the people and taking their large entrenched camp at Sigiburg. He then marched into Engria, reconquered the mid-Saxons, and crossed the river Weser into Eastphalia. It was the Eastphalian tribes who first did homage to Charles, accepting Christianity; they were soon followed by the Engrians, and hostages were taken as security for the oaths made. The Westphalians were more difficult to subdue, however, and Charles ravaged their territory, slaughtering the warriors and people ruthlessly. Upon their submission, the Westphalians were held in check by garrisons at two large Frankish camps, at Eresburg and Sigiburg. Many hostages from the families of tribal chiefs were taken, mainly youths who were deposited in Christian monasteries in Austrasia, Charles' homeland territory. As a result of this first extensive conquest of Saxony, three-quarters of the Saxons did homage to Charles, but not for long.

Second Conquest of Saxony

As might be guessed from the nature of the Saxons and their land, Charles was soon forced to return and re-establish his supremacy. In 776, when the Frankish army set out on the second invasion of Italy to quell the rebellious supporters of Prince Adelchis, the Westphalians and Engrians revolted.

The camp at Eresburg was taken and the garrison put to death, but the camp at Sigiburg held out. When Charles heard this news, and we must remember that even the fastest military courier might take weeks to bring such a message, he returned to Saxony with astonishing speed, taking the Saxons by surprise.

The shock of Charles and his army appearing suddenly when they were supposed to be usefully employed in far distant Italy filled the Saxons with fear, and they sued for peace. The leaders accepted baptism for themselves and their people, and promised to hold their lands as vassals of the Frankish king. Thus Saxony was conquered for a second time.

One chieftain, Wittikind, fled north to take refuge with the Danes, a race hardly known to the Franks at that time, but who would later make inroads into the empire. The garrison at Eresburg was replaced, and Charles ordered the construction of another entrenched camp at Karlstadt. He then remained in Austrasia for the winter, keeping close to the Saxon border, ready for further insurrection.

The following spring Charles called a great council at Paderborn, in the centre of Engria, to confirm that Saxony was now indeed part of the Frankish realm. Many Saxons were baptised and swore oaths to remain loyal, on threat of forfeiture of their lands and freedom.

The great council at Paderborn was also attended by ambassadors from Saracen Spain, with a surprising offer of homage from Soliman Ibn-al-Arabi and Kasmin Ibn-Yussuf. These chiefs held the north-eastern towns of Barcelona, Huseca and Gerona, close to Charles' border. They proposed that they became Frankish vassals in return for protection against the expanding might of Abd-ar-Rahman the Ommeyad, who had taken over virtually the whole of Spain.

Charles, thinking that Saxony was now safely secured, accepted this offer, which effectively pushed his own frontier beyond the Pyrenees. In 778 he led a huge army into Spain.

Invasion of Spain

Charles led an army of Neustrians over the western Pyrenees, while a further force levied from Austrasia, Lombardy and Burgundy, crossed

the eastern Pyrenees. Before Saragossa the two Frankish hosts joined together, and the king received homage from those Saracen chiefs who had invited him into Spain as their protector.

However, Saragossa could not be taken, despite the vast forces set against it and Charles decided to return to Aquitaine, having gained very little other than the defeat of the Basques after storming Pamplona. Neither the Saracen vassals nor the Basque and Navarese vassals were trustworthy, and in 778 while the army was returning across the Pyrenees, Basque warriors attacked the wagon train, capturing considerable amounts of booty and killing three senior members of Charles' government. This was the background to one of the most famous incidents of heroism in early literature, for the pass was Ronscevalles and

The fall of Pamplona, from a detail on Charlemagne's tomb at Aachen. He is seen on his knees, whilst God shatters the wall held by the defending Moslem forces.

31

the dead men were Eggihard the Seneschal, Anselm, Count of the Palace, and Roland, Warden of the Breton Marches. Very little is known historically about Roland, but his fame lives on in the *Chanson de Roland* and legends that arose not long after his heroic death.

Upon reaching Aquitaine after this defeat at the hands of the Basques, Charles was informed that the Saxons had uprisen yet again. Wittikind, who had not sworn fealty to Charles, had returned from his exile in Denmark to arouse his countrymen and a huge Saxon host had attacked the fort at Karlstadt, taking revenge for the destruction of the sacred *Irminsul* and Charles' other ravages of Saxony. Churches were burned, priests and peasants put to death, and the Saxon nationalists (if they may be called such) were further strengthened by the fact that Charles did not muster a Frankish army until the summer of 779.

The by now familiar pattern repeated itself; Westphalia was finally put to fire and sword by the avenging Franks, and the Westphalians were defeated. The Eastphalians and Engrians submitted without giving battle, and Charles retired to consider how he might best keep the Saxons under submission.

Fourth Conquest of Saxony

In the spring of 780, Charles ordered a council or diet at the head of the River Lippe, and initiated a plan for the control of Saxony. The entire land was to be divided into missionary territories, each division under the religious instruction of a group of monks from Austrasia.

This division was aimed at establishing regular bishoprics which combined secular and religious political control; such bishoprics would be part of the state system of government along with minor kingships, dukes, counts and other nobles and officials. Once again, Charles proved the effectiveness of Christianity as a tool of suppression; there seems little doubt that it was the only possible way to control the Saxons. Many thousands of pagans were baptised and Charles himself is recorded as assisting in mass baptism in the rivers Elbe and Ocker in 780.

Between 780 and 782 Saxony seemed to be well under control; even when Charles left the country, no immediate rebellion occurred, and enforced missionary work seemed to be successful. Once again, it was fear of Charles and his military might that converted the Saxons, not love of Christ (who must have seemed to them a very hard, vengeful god indeed).

As a result of this progress, Charles divided Saxony into countships for civil rule, giving office not only to Frankish favourites and able governors, but also to Saxon chieftains. This moderate system of government was frequently adopted by Charles, who early on in his reign had recognised the wisdom of leaving local leaders in place wherever it seemed possible and beneficial to his own aims. A Saxon code of law was published, which dealt firmly with reversions to

Frankish soldiers commit a terrible mass execution of defiant Saxons at Verden. Charlemagne's order of the beheading of 4,500 bound prisoners earned him the Saxon's bitter hatred for many years.

paganism; any return to the old way of worship was punished by death. Crimes specified were robbing churches, burning instead of burying the dead, deriding Christian services and practices, and sacrificing to Woden. The death penalty could also be applied to those who refused baptism, failed to conform to ecclesiastical disciplines given out by missionary leaders, or who refused to fast in Lent. Fines could also be imposed.

The Massacre of Verden

By 782, in response to this increased formalising and application of militant Christianity, Wittikind returned again from his refuge in pagan Denmark and summoned the northern tribes to revolt. Once again Charles applied superior force, and many of the rebels immediately submitted. But churches had been burnt, priests killed, and proud Saxons had ritually washed off their enforced baptism. Charles resolved upon a severe punishment.

The most active rebel leaders and warriors were brought as captives to Charles on his command; 4,500 men were bound and taken by their countrymen to a camp at Verden on the River Aller. Charles ordered the beheading of the entire company, bound and helpless as they were.

Once again the Saxons showed their spirit, and rose *en masse* to avenge this cruel execution. Even the most obliging and servile tribes took arms against Charles; the matter was now one of a blood feud as well as a religious war. Between 783 and 785 there was continual conflict across Saxony. Charles swept the land twice with his armies, burning and killing wherever he could find victims, but the Saxons held out in the impenetrable forests and marshes, closing in behind the Frankish military movements.

In the winter of 784 Charles and his army remained in Minden in the middle of Saxony, an unusual move designed to weaken the rebels, who were accustomed to 'the great king' leaving their land each winter.

Fifth Conquest of Saxony

In 785 Charles' inflexible attitude and persistent presence finally paid off; the main nationalist leader, Wittikind, sued for peace and was given his life in exchange for his surrender and baptism. When Wittikind and his warriors capitulated, the revolt began to collapse. Charles reinstated his counts, rebuilt his churches, installed new priests, and the Saxons found themselves back under Frankish control.

Between 785 and 792, Frankish rule was consolidated in Saxony. There were four further uprisings between 792 and 804, but these occurred in a Saxony that was already well under control and were readily crushed. In 788 Charles replaced his vassal Tassilo, Duke of Bavaria, with the effective countship system of government. The disloyal Duke, who had frequently been rebellious, was exiled to the

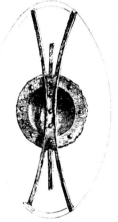

The umbo or boss of a Frankish shield from below and in profile. Early archaeology mistook these for helmets.

Charlemagne's baggage train is attacked whilst crossing the Alps on one of his campaigns. Massive baggage trains enabled rapid troop movement by the Frankish army without repeated foraging.

Neustrian monastery of Jumieges. With this annexation of Bavaria, Charles completed his conquest of the Saxons and the Germans and he now turned his attention to other regions bordering upon his extensive kingdom.

Extending the Kingdom

From around 785 to 814 Charles entered into a second stage of his expansion and conquests. During this period we find him in conflict with races who were very different to the Franks: the Slavs and Avars in the east and the Saracens in the south and west. He also came into conflict with the Empire of the East, an orthodox Christian empire with territories touching upon those of Italy, with many differences and oppositions to papal and Frankish interests.

During the second phase of expansion, Charles allocated authority to his three sons; each had a kingdom under Charles, and was expected to guard the borders against hostile invasion. The eldest son, another Charles, ruled western Neustria, which consisted of Anjou, Maine and Touraine. The second son, named Pepin after his grandfather, ruled Lombardy. Ludovic or Louis, the youngest, ruled Aquitaine.

Thus Louis controlled the frontier with the Saracens in the Pyrenees, Pepin curtailed the Duke of Benevento and defended north-eastern Italy against incursions by the Avars, and Charles the Younger fought against the Bretons of Armorica, who rebelled in 786 and 799 against Frankish rule.

In addition to fixed territories and frontier duties, the sons were also employed by their father on specific campaigns in other territories. Pepin directed campaigns against the Slavs in Bohemia; Louis conducted campaigns in southern Italy, though he was by no means a military leader by nature; and Charles the Younger led forces against the Saxons in his father's name.

It seems to have been Charles' policy to broaden the education and leadership of his sons, and at the same time not to allow them to become too entrenched in their own subkingdoms. In addition to the mobility required of them as deputies in battle for the king, they were also kept in attendance at their father's court at Aachen for long periods of time. It was partly this prudent use of his sons that enabled Charles to expand, control and defend his kingdom upon many fronts at once.

Subjugation of the Slavs
The far north-eastern border of Charles' kingdom joined upon the

territories of various Slavonic tribes. They were a primitive and tribal people, and do not seem to have been such fierce opponents as the Saxons. The main tribes, as mentioned earlier were the Abotrites, the Sorbs and the Wiltzes, ruled by various chiefs and tribal princes who were not unified in their opposition to the Franks.

Charles crossed the River Elbe in 789 with an army of Franks, Frisians and Saxons. The Saxons were fighting the Slavs as ancestral enemies and so were an excellent choice; furthermore they were increasingly absorbed into Charles' system of government, and would have to guard the borders upon his departure. The Slav opposition collapsed almost immediately, as if the very name of Charles had struck terror into their hearts.

Witzin, King of the Abotrites, and Dragovit, King of the Wiltzes did homage to Charles, paid tribute and gave hostages. More important for the long-term programme of submission was the fact that they agreed to allow Christian missionaries into their lands. The Frankish army secured most of the northern territories, and the Slavs kept their word to Charles. In 795 they aided the Franks against rebellious Saxons, and in 798 the King of the Abotrites actually conquered Nordalbingian rebels, captured their leader and brought him to Charles. Within a decade most of the Slavs were fighting Danish invaders on behalf of the Frankish Empire.

Conflict with the Avars

In 805–6 Charles sent his eldest son against the Czechs of Bohemia. Charles the Younger wasted the region of the Upper Elbe so thoroughly that the Czechs submitted, and agreed to pay tribute to the Franks.

Along the rivers Danube, Raab and Leithe, to the south of Bohemia, Charles' borders were fringed by the Avars. These were a Tartar people who had been traditional enemies of the Lombards and the Eastern Empire at Constantinople for generations. In 788 the Avars invaded the Lombard territory of Fruili and the Duchy of Bavaria, both under Charles' rule. The days of immediate response and speedy marches were over for Charles with such a complex and expanding realm to govern; two years passed before he invaded the Avar lands in retribution.

Charles led an Austrasian and Saxon army personally down the Danube, and wasted Avar territories as far as the River Raab. Simultaneously a huge Lombard army marched through the valley of the Drave into the middle of Pannonia. This host defeated the Avars in battle and stormed their camps. It seemed likely that the Avars would be subjected to Frankish rule, but revolt in Saxony called Charles away. For the following two campaigning seasons Charles subdued Saxons. In fact, he did not personally lead forces against the Avars again.

His son Pepin, aided by Eric of Fruili, now led the campaign in Charles' absence. They captured the Avars royal circular camp and sent great booty to Aachen. There was so much spoil from this Avar stronghold that Charles used it as gifts, and it was some of of this booty that reached the distant King Offa of Mercia, in central Britain.

Eventually the Avars did homage to Charles; their *tuduns* or chieftains came to Aachen and were baptised. In 805 Charles chose one chieftain to reign as his vassal king, and bestowed upon him the ancient title of Chagan, which had originally been that of the independent High King of the Avars. Upon baptism this king took the Christian name of Abraham – perhaps because he hoped to be the father of a long line of kings associated with Frankish power.

To the south of the Avars, the Bavarian and Lombard forces also subdued the Slavs of Drave and Save. Known as Carinthians and Slovenians, these tribes, at one time vassals of the original Avar Chagans, now paid tribute to Charles, though they were not fully absorbed into the Frankish realm or system of government.

The Eastern Empire, Italy and Spain

In Italy, control eventually devolved to Pepin, the second son of Charles. As described, he had to contain the troublesome region of Benevento, but another power also held parts of southern Italy, the Eastern Empire based at Constantinople.

The Diadem Crown of Charlemagne now held in Vienna.

Charlemagne's stone throne in the Octagon at Aachen Cathedral. Originally, this symbolic seat of power contained holy relics.

Eastern Imperial territories in Italy included Naples, Brindisi and Reggio, with homage from the independent states of Venice and Istria. For much of Charles' reign Constantinople was under the control of relatively ineffectual rulers, and had many internal disputes and factions which made imperial interest in Italy difficult to enforce. Between 780–790 and 797–802, the Empress Irene ruled, a matter which was regarded with much scorn, fear and loathing by the European Church. Then from 802–811 the unsurper Nicephorus I held the throne. This unstable situation did not prevent intense imperial resentment of Charles' growing power.

When Charles was eventually declared Emperor of the West in 800 the Eastern Empire regarded this (perhaps correctly) as usurpation of a title that belonged to Constantinople. To a certain extent the East Romans, as they were still called, were genuine heirs to the original Roman Empire, their capital having been founded by Constantine the Great in 324–340. The Franks, on the other hand, were the heirs of the barbarians who had destroyed the Roman Empire in the West.

As we have seen, Constantinople gave refuge to Prince Adelchis (son of Charles' first father-in-law, Desiderius), who still maintained op-

37

position to Charles in Italy, albeit from afar. But between 804 and 810, Nicephorus I commanded a series of expeditions against Italy, for Venice had transferred her homage to Charles. Nicephorus' fleet harried the accessible southern coasts in retribution, but made no firm gains. Then when a pro-East Roman party gained control of Venice, allegiance was declared in favour of Nicephorus once again, and peace was made with Charles.

As a result of these disputes, Charles gained possession of a number of Istrian coastal cities which had originally been under the rule of Constantinople. In 812 Nicephorus was succeeded by Michael Rhangabe, who recognised Charles as Emperor of the West, despite much opposition from his own people. It seemed clear that the Franks were a power in Europe that the Eastern Empire did not dare to challenge on a large scale.

Expansion into Spain

As the boundaries of Charles' dominions extended southwards in Italy, he came into conflict with the Saracens, who were widespread in the Mediterranean. When Charles took Corsica and Sardinia, he drove out Saracens who had taken these islands, in turn, from the East Romans. In 799 the Franks took the Balearic Islands, which faced repeated attacks from Saracen fleets, but were held under the government of the Counts of Genoa and Tuscany.

In Spain there was unbroken war with the Saracens. In 785 the Franks advanced over the Pyrenees and took Genoa; internal dissent between rival Moslem factions helped Charles' gradual conquest of Spain, but it was no easy task. The Spanish wars were led by Louis, Charles' third son, now King of Aquitaine. His chief councillor and military leader was William of Toulouse, one of the great Frankish heroes. It seems likely, judging from Louis' later life, that the military effort was mainly conducted by William, for the King of Aquitaine was inclined more to the cloister and altar than the sword and buckler.

Saracen opposition came from two powerful Ommayad kings of Cordova: Abd ar-Rahman (756–788) and Hisham (788–807). As a result of rebellion by their own Moslem vassals, to whom religious unity was less important than political power, these rulers were frequently faced by Frankish armies called in as allies by the rebels. In 795 Charles created the territory of the March of Spain, incorporating those gains made beyond the Pyrenees and including Ausona, Cardona, Gerona and Urgel. In 797 Barcelona, the main Catelonian city, fell to the Franks and the Saracen governor, Zeid, rebelling against his master in Cordova, sought vassalage with the Christians rather than defeat at the hands of a fellow Moslem.

In 799 the Moors retook Barcelona, and King Louis of Aquitaine laid siege to it. It finally fell two years later as a result of famine, having been surrounded by Frankish earthworks and troops who had remained

Decorated hunting horn reputed to have belonged to Charlemagne.

through the winter months. After this second surrender of Barcelona the Moorish population was removed, and the city repopulated with people from Septimania, thus ensuring that further racial and religious ties would not weaken this important stronghold in Spain. Charles now proceeded to push the Frankish border further south.

In 809 Tarragona fell, and in 811 Charles took the important fortress of Tortosa, which controlled the lower part of the river Ebro. From there the Franks crossed over into Valencia, where they did extensive damage. In 812 the third Ommeyad ruler in Cordova, Al-Hakem, sought terms with Charles. It must have seemed clear to him that the Frankish advance could not be stopped by armed opposition, for he ceded to Charles all the territories gained across the Pyrenees. In later years Barcelona and the region to the north formed part of the kingdom of Arragon, and acted as a buffer against Saracen invasions into the rest of Europe.

Final Saxon Campaigns

In 792 the Saxons revolted yet again; this time it took two years of campaigning to suppress the Eastphalians and Nordalbingians involved. It is interesting that Charles' army now consisted in part of Christianised Saxons and Abotrite Slavs.

As late as 804 the northernmost Saxon tribes revolted once more, and on this occasion Charles resorted to deportation as a cure. Ten thousand Nordalbingian families, effectively the whole race, were transported to Gaul, and settled in small colonies among the Neustrians, many as slaves. The depopulated territories were given to Charles' loyal vassal, the King of the Abotrites. This massive forced deportation concluded Charles' conquest of Saxony, for as a chronicler records 'henceforth they abandoned worship of evil spirits, and gave up the wicked customs of their forefathers, received the sacrament of Chrisitan baptism, mingling with the Franks until at last they were reckoned as one race . . .'

Between 804 and 806 Charles placed bishops at Munster, Bremen and Paderborn (in north, west and south Saxony). It was this establishment of bishoprics that finally destroyed Saxon identity, for life began to revolve around centralised locations with the bishoprics generating towns, and the ancient semi-nomadic life was eroded.

Conflict with the Danes

As already described, the Saxon rebel Wittikind fled to the Danes for protection during the second conquest of Saxony in 776. By 808 the Danes were fully aware of the danger of Frankish expansion, and their king, Godfred, built a massive earthwork along his frontier. The *Dannewerk* at the narrowest point of the isthmus of Schleswig, reached from sea to sea, and remained as a strategic position in wars between Danes and Germans until as late as the nineteenth century.

The Danes also began to attack and raid along the Flemish and Frisian coasts, reaching as far south as the mouth of the Seine. They also attacked Charles' Slavonic subjects on the Baltic. King Godfred made extensive forays into Frisia, and subdued the Abotrites and Wiltzes. His tactic was simple: he harried the coastline wherever it was not heavily guarded, and simply withdrew by sea when Frankish opposition appeared. In 810 he even boasted that he might visit Charles in Aachen, as he had already made deep inroads into Frisia. This threat was never to be fulfilled, for Godfred was conveniently murdered, and his successor and nephew, Hemming, made peace with the Franks.

Emperor of the West

Strictly speaking, the original Roman Empire survived only in Constantinople as the 'East Romans', separate from Rome itself in culture, and, for some periods, in interpretation and practice of Christian religion. There had not been an *Augustus* or Western Emperor for centuries, but the concept remained, and papal authority tended to repudiate Constantinople, even without a Western Emperor. When the Empress Irene took the Eastern throne, Rome refused to recognise her authority. The scene was already set for Charles to become a new Western Emperor.

In 800 Pope Leo III was taken prisoner by relatives of his predecessor Hadrian I. They tried to blind him, but he escaped and fled over the Alps to Charles, who was encamped at Paderborn in central Saxony. Charles resolved to travel to Rome to settle the feud, and gave Leo the protection of Frankish warriors to return home in the meantime. Towards the end of the year Charles travelled to Rome himself, and held a synod to investigate the matter. Not surprisingly, Leo was found innocent and his enemies were executed or imprisoned; after a ceremonial oath taking, Leo III was reinstated as Pope.

By this time the festival of Christmas had arrived, and both papal and royal courts joined together to celebrate in St Peter's basilica. At the close of the service, while Charles knelt in prayer, Leo placed a diadem on the king's head and pronounced: 'God grant life and victory to Charles the Augustus, crowned by God great and pacific Emperor of the Romans'. This theatrical cry was taken up by the assembled Franks and Romans, and all present, including the pope, prostrated themselves before Charles in the ancient manner reserved for Emperor of Rome.

We might think, in retrospect, that it was a set piece of rather obvious connivance; Charles ruled Europe in any case, and his elevation to emperor seemed to solve the problem of the notorious Empress Irene in Constantinople. But there were no legal precedents for a barbarian emperor, and certainly no precedents for the imperial power being bestowed by a pope.

Charles stated that he did not know what was to take place, and would not have entered St Peter's basilica if he had known. Like other monarchs through history, Charles took the course of letting another take the most major step on his behalf; if it went wrong he could repudiate it, if it went well then it was obviously a wise action for all. There was little doubt that the crowning, vexed with political and religious implications and problems as it was, had popular approval.

The name of emperor had ceased among the Greeks (of Constantinople) for they were enduring the reign of a woman, wherefore it seemed good both to Leo the apostolic Pope, and to the holy fathers in council with him, and to all Christian men, that they should hail Charles king of the Franks as emperor. For he held Rome itself, where the ancient Caesars had always dwelt, and all those other possessions of his own in Italy,

These fourteenth-century miniatures from the Chroniques de Saint Denis *depict (left) Charlemagne's coronation by Pope Leo III and (right) 'Charlemagne's Vision'.*

41

Gaul, and Germany. Wherefore as God had granted him all these dominions, it seemed just to them that he should accept the imperial title also, when it was offered to him by the consent of all Christendom.

(Chronicle of Lauresheim)

The Pope implied that apostolic or divine inspiration had led to the crowning, Charles was therefore 'crowned by God'. This side-stepped the legal aspects of the coronation, for the combined nations of Europe might have chosen to elect an emperor by some other means – though undoubtedly this person would have been Charles. In the long term the crowning of Charles by Leo III led to an increasing papal claim to power over the imperial ruler of the West, but short-term benefits to Charles were clear. In addition to being elected King of the Franks, and overlord of vast territories in Europe, Charles was now divinely crowned. He did not hesitate to emphasise his authority in religious matters, which were already such an integral part of his system of government.

Imperial Rule

After the dramatic crowning of Charles – the first and last time that a pope paid homage to the new Emperors of the West – came a period of reinforcement of his new status. Charles made his subjects swear a new form of allegiance to him as emperor, the vow being administered to all people over the age of twelve:

His vow of homage was not merely a promise to be true to the emperor and to serve him against his enemies, but a promise to live in obedience to God and His law according to the best of each man's strength and understanding. It was a vow to abstain from theft and oppression and injustice, no less than from heathen practices and witchcraft; a vow to do no wrong to the Churches of God, nor to injure widows and orphans, of whom the emperor is the chosen protector and guardian.

Thus law, religion and mortality were all bound up in the imperial title and role, and any offence against the Emperor and his law was an offence directly against God. It is from this carefully defined power base that the concept of the Holy Roman Empire began – a concept that was to have a profound effect upon European history.

The extensive military conquests had been turned, through one ritual act in Rome, into a spiritual empire, with church and state unified under the control of a reigning emperor. The ultimate image was perhaps one of benevolent religious despotism, with the ruler under divine blessing taking care of all members of his realm. It was never realised as such, of course, and the conflict for supremacy between popes and kings took centuries to resolve. Initially, the effect of Leo III crowning Charles was to greatly strengthen papal power, though this was not fully apparent until after Charles' death.

Division of the Empire

In 806 Charles declared the future division of his empire. Upon his death the title of Emperor, the Frankish territories of Austrasia and Neustria, plus Saxony, Burgundy and Thuringia, would go to his eldest son Charles. His second son Pepin would rule Italy, Bavaria and eastern Suabia. Louis (later to be known as 'the Pious') would rule the Spanish March, Aquitaine and Provence. Such division among sons was traditional to the Franks, and comprised an important part of their ancient, mainly unwritten, code of laws.

However, both Charles the Younger and Pepin died within one year of each other, the eldest in 811, his brother in 810. Suddenly Louis was heir to a vast realm that excluded only Italy, which was to be a vassal kingdom for Pepin's son Bernard.

The Death of Charles

Charles died on the 28th January 814, after complications following a winter cold. He was buried in the cathedral at Aachen, in a sacrophagus taken from an ancient Roman site somewhere in Italy. A golden shrine was placed over his tomb, with an image of Charles and the simple inscription:

Sub hoc conditorio situm est corpus Karoli Magni et orthodoxi imperatoris, qui regnum francorum nobiliter apliavit, et per annos xlvii feliciter rexit.

Within this tomb is laid the body of the Christian Emperor Charlemagne, who guided the kingdom of the Franks with distinction and ruled it with success for 47 years.

(trans: Colin Stockford)

The Charlemagne Legacy

The achievements of Charles the Great were comprehensive: in addition to advances in religion, law and military rule during his reign, he worked extensively to develop learning within his empire. However, one must realise that religion, law, rule and learning were fused together in the consciousness of the eighth and ninth centuries. Charles worked very hard indeed to strengthen this fusion, under the single role of emperor, as leader of all human endeavour and development.

Cultural Achievements

Charles made serious efforts to develop the learning and culture of his court and society. He summoned scholars and men of wisdom from all over the known world, his main personal tutor and mentor being Alcuin of Northumberland from England. Alcuin taught Charles dialectic and rhetoric, while grammar was taught by Peter of Pisa. In encouraging scholars to attend his palace, Charlemagne allowed a freedom of speech which would have been unthinkable from other men. Alcuin argued openly with him over subjects such as the enforced baptism of Saxons. We may see in this encouragement of scholars not only an attempt to improve the status of the realm, but a genuine curiosity for learning on the part of Charles himself. These scholars taught the 'liberal arts' which Charles sought to learn and instill in his court; they do not correspond to our modern subjects of the same name, but have a wider philosophical and metaphysical basis.

Like most rulers in the Dark Ages and the later Medieval and Renaissance periods, Charles paid attention to the patterns of the stars and planets; he studied the astronomy of the time, which was unified with astrology and philosophy based upon the Four Elements (Air, Fire, Water, Earth). He even devised new German names for the twelve winds and the twelve months of the year, showing a depth of interest and love of order that far exceeds mere military might and cunning. It was this vision of order that held his vast empire together and on his death the entire vision collapsed, and the realm rapidly fell into decay and disunity.

In a practical sense, he encouraged and demanded higher standards of literacy from his churchmen and governors, and issued various proclamations condemning their ignorance of Latin. Schools were started in the monasteries, for Charles proclaimed that 'Men of God should not only live by the rule and dwell in holy conversation, but should devote themselves to literary meditations, each according to his ability, that they may be able to give themselves to the duty of teaching others.'

He even learned to write himself, an art normally left to professional scribes and often despised by members of the militaristic nobility. His signature is preserved to this day on documents. Unfortunately, he was already an adult when he took up writing, and did not become fluent. Nevertheless we are told that he kept tablets or notebooks under his pillow, and would practise his letters from time to time. It is worth considering that hands long formed to the sword, reins, shield and other military accoutrements become stiffened and calloused and it may be that the use of a small stylus or quill was physically difficult for Charles; we can be in no doubt about his energy and intelligence.

Charles also concerned himself with building, and actually helped to design his major cathedral at Aachen, part of which remains today. In the construction marble was brought from Ravenna and Rome, probably taken from earlier Roman works, and bronze rails and doors were cast, with many golden and silver lamps. Church building was also a notable aspect of Charles' government.

Under Charles, the monasteries developed as centres of learning, but he also instigated a programme of reforms of literature, particularly in preservation and copying. Under his instructions, many classical texts were recopied from worn out manuscripts; monasteries were encouraged to make multiple copies of their libraries, and to exchange texts with one another.

Aachen Cathedral (opposite) as it appears today is built around Charlemagne's original chapel and the city still bears the French name of Aix-la-Chapelle.

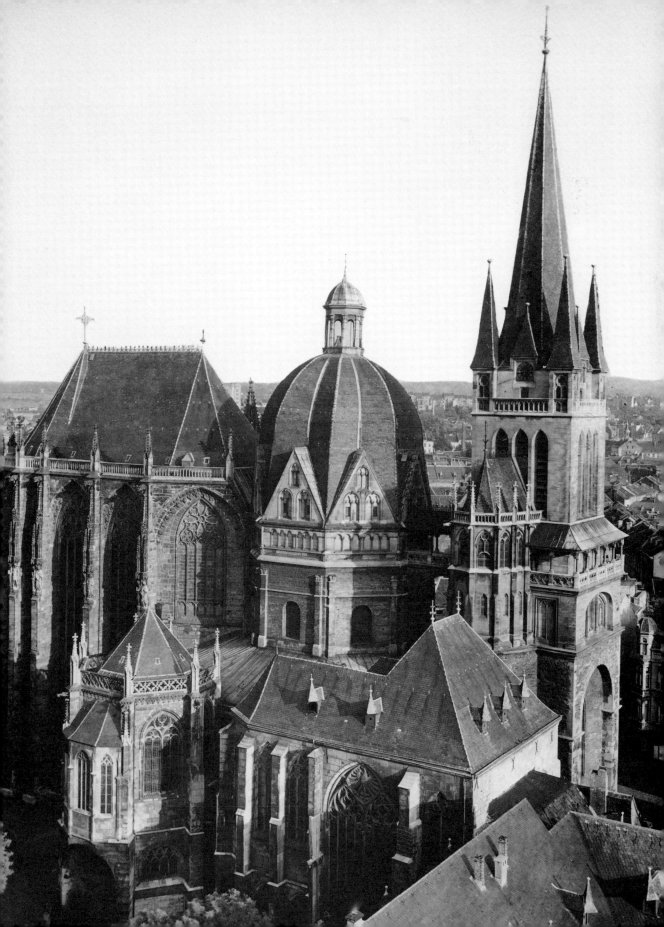

The conquest of Jerusalem as shown in the fifteenth-century Chroniques de Charlemagne.

Charles discovered that there were many variant readings of the Testaments, due to the ignorance of copyists. One of his great scholars, Paul the Deacon, was given the task of preparing a new lectionary (list of lessons for reading), drawn from the best selected texts. This definitive version was to be used in all churches throughout the realm. Traditional epics taken from Frankish oral poetry also commanded Charles' interest, and he had several of these copied out into formal texts. Grammars of Latin and German were assembled by scholars, plus biographies (which formed a major part of medieval literature) and works of history.

Charles' reign was a major turning point in the development of literary records; prior to his time, records were vague and often confusing. Oral tradition played a major role in education, and we we should remember that many of Charles' legal documents were merely written reminders which related to verbal laws, decisions, commands and traditions.

But his rejuvenation of religious and, to a lesser extent, secular, texts and libraries was the first major effort at establishing a corpus of learning in the West on the part of a king since the collapse of the original Roman state. Even styles of handwriting were improved radically, giving clear texts and defined forms.

The main gathering of scholars was at Charles' court, and it seems clear that there was a conscious attempt to restore classical glories, even though much of this did not percolate far beyond the royal circle of intimates. Charles was known as 'King David', and Alcuin as 'Flaccus', while other scholars took the names of Homer, Mopsus and other classical writers. This use of nicknames may seem rather contrived to the

46

modern mind, but allegory, riddling, connective names and patterns, were an integral part of the literature, consciousness and style of the period. Scholars such as Alcuin composed verses with many hidden references or acrostic patterns, and while they may seem trivial today, they represented a quest for pattern, meaning and subtle order, and were not mere exercises in wittiness.

Charles also patronised music and encouraged Italian masters to teach Gregorian chant to the wild choristers of the Frankish and Saxon realms. Art also began to take a distinctive style and many surviving examples combine elements of subtlety, barbaric splendour and beauty. In Aachen, Charles built not only a formal palace, but a huge basilica, some of which was incorporated into what is now the present cathedral.

Depiction of the legendary coronation of Charles in Jerusalem, an example of religiously inspired fiction which also appears in the Chroniques de Charlemagne.

Permanence of Legend

Palaces were constructed in the ancient Austrasian royal centres, and Charles instigated the first major bridge building for centuries, with a structure 500 metres long at Mainz. Although this bridge was destroyed by fire on 813 and not restored, part of another immense feat of engineering remains today in the abandoned canal intended to join the Rhine and Danube.

So great were such feats, and so very great was Charles, that countless legends sprung up around him, and his rule began to be thought of as a golden age. Both the Germans and the French claim him as a hero, and in this sense the Emperor becomes more than a mortal ruler. Like King Arthur of the Britons, Charles the Great, *Caroli Magni*, changed from being a historical person into a legendary ideal – the great ruler who set the world aright, and encouraged men and women to live by a fusion of spiritual and material principles.

Unlike many of his time, Charlemagne had the skill of writing, as in his imperial signature on a document dated 775.

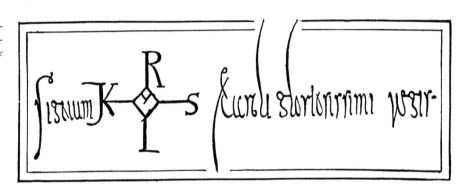

Bibliography

Buckler, F.W. *Harun 'il Rashid and Charles the Great* Cambridge, Mass, 1931.

Bullough, D. *The Age of Charlemagne*, London and New York, 1965.

Fichtenau, H. *The Carolingian Empire* London and New York, 1954.

Heer, F. *Charlemagne and his World* Weidenfeld & Nicolson, London, 1975.

Lamb, H.A. *Charlemagne* London, 1962.

Montgomery Watt, W. *A History of Islamic Spain* Edinburgh, 1965.

Owen, D.D.R. *The Legend of Roland* London and New York, 1973.

Riche, P. *Daily Life in the World of Charlemagne* Liverpool, 1978.

Thompson, A.E. *The Early Germans* Oxford, 1965.

Thorpe, L. (trans). *Einhard and Notker the Stammerer: Two Lives of Charlemagne* Penguin, London, 1969.

GENEALOGY OF CHARACTERS

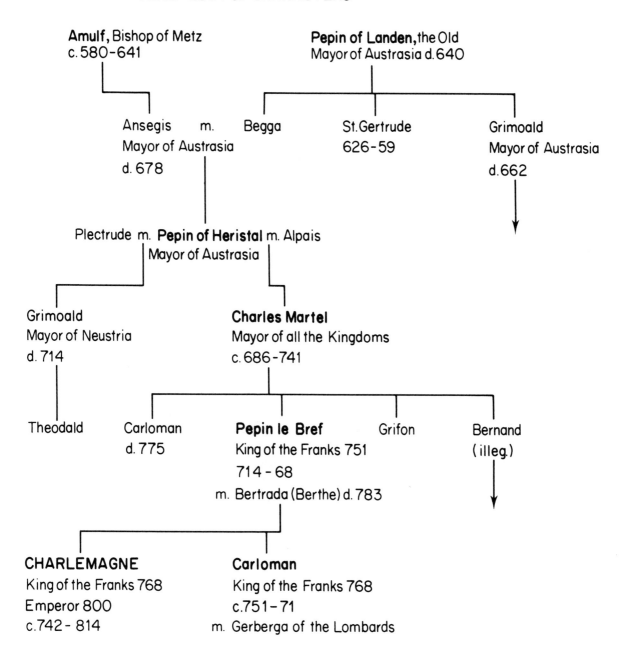

Arnulf, Bishop of Metz
c. 580-641

Pepin of Landen, the Old
Mayor of Austrasia d. 640

Ansegis   m.   Begga
Mayor of Austrasia
d. 678

St. Gertrude
626-59

Grimoald
Mayor of Austrasia
d. 662

Plectrude m. **Pepin of Heristal** m. Alpais
Mayor of Austrasia

Grimoald
Mayor of Neustria
d. 714

Charles Martel
Mayor of all the Kingdoms
c. 686-741

Theodald

Carloman
d. 775

Pepin le Bref
King of the Franks 751
714-68
m. Bertrada (Berthe) d. 783

Grifon

Bernand
(illeg.)

CHARLEMAGNE
King of the Franks 768
Emperor 800
c. 742-814

Carloman
King of the Franks 768
c. 751-71
m. Gerberga of the Lombards

CHAMPION OF SPAIN

THE SPAIN OF EL CID

DUCHIES OF
AQUITAINE
AND POITIERS

THE FRANKS

Santiago ASTURIAS •Oviedo

GALICIA

Kingdom of
Navarre and Aragon
(Sancho Ramires)

•Leon Bivar •

Kingdom of Leon and Castille • Burgos
(Alfonso VI)

Kingdom of
Saragossa
(Mostain 1085–1101
El Cid 1081–87)

PORTUGAL Zamora • CHRISTIAN SPAIN

Salamanca • • Segovia

Toledo •

Kingdom of Badajoz
(Omar Motawakkil)

MOSLEM SPAIN

Kingdom of Seville
(Ben Abbed Motamid) Kingdom of Granada
(Abdallah)
• Granada

Gibraltar

Tangier Ceuta

El Cid Campeador – Rodrigo del Bivar

He was Rodrigo del Bivar – otherwise known as El Cid or 'the Lord' – one of the most complex and remarkable heroes of the Middle Ages. In his most familiar guise, as a literary figure, he is brave, heroic, loyal, a good husband and father, a redoubtable foe and a man of honour. In short, he is all that a medieval paladin might be expected to be. However, even within that most famous and partisan account of his life, the twelfth century *Poema del Cid*, there is an element of cunning, almost knavish behaviour which is far from usual in such a character. El Cid lies, cheats, even steals from innocent men; while elsewhere the portrait is even less flattering.

Yet despite all this, El Cid is probably Spain's greatest hero. He is famed for his just behaviour, nobility and magnanimity. He was so respected by his natural enemies, the Moors, that when he was exiled by his Christian overlords, they were more than willing to give him shelter and employment. Indeed, it was the Moors who gave him the title by which he is best known, a contraction of the Arabic *sid-y*, meaning 'my lord'.

He was born in 1043 at Bivar, a village to the north of Burgos in northern Spain. As the son of noble parents, Rodrigo was brought up and trained in knightly pursuits at the court of Prince Sancho, eldest son of King Ferdinand of Castile and Leon. He soon proved himself a redoubtable warrior, and won the respect of his peers. When, with the death of Ferdinand in 1065, civil war broke out between his surviving sons, Rodrigo commanded the army of his overlord Prince Sancho.

Then, in 1077, Sancho was murdered and El Cid became a favourite at the court of his brother Alfonso and his sister Urraca. There was believed to have been an incestuous relationship between Alfonso and Urraca and they were probably responsible for Sancho's death. Whether or not he suspected this, Rodrigo accepted the favours bestowed upon him by the new King – including marriage to Alfonso's niece Ximena Diaz.

It seems to have been a happy marriage and Ximena bore Rodrigo two daughters. But Rodrigo had made many enemies, both among the disgraced followers of the murdered Sancho (who saw his change of

allegiancies as disaster) and those at the court of Alfonso (who saw his rise as a threat). In particular, the powerful Beni-Gomez family schemed continually against Rodrigo until Alfonso banished him in 1081.

It was from this point that Rodrigo's life as a wandering and heroic adventurer began in earnest. He gathered a considerable following of loyal and disaffected men, and together they served many masters, both Christian and Moslem, during the next five years.

Then, in 1095, a new influx of Moorish invaders landed in Spain. They were led by a fanatical chieftain named Yusuf and Alfonso was soundly defeated at the battle of Sagrajas. Rodrigo, by now widely known as El Cid Campeador (the battler), was recalled to favour and proceeded at once to drive back the invaders. This he did with such success that within the next few years his name became a byword throughout Spain.

From then until his death in 1099 at the age of fifty-six, El Cid fought a series of dazzling campaigns against the Moors, taking the fortified city of Valencia and making it an impregnable fortress against his enemies When news of his death reached the rest of Spain, men and women wept openly in the streets, tearing their clothing and lacerating their cheeks in an extravagent display of mourning.

Many refused to believe El Cid was actually dead. Just as with other heroes like Arthur and Charlemagne, it was thought that he had been transported to another time or place to await his country's greatest need. The legend of El Cid began there, but nearly a thousand years were to pass before the true story of his life and deeds began to be known.

Eleventh Century Spain

El Cid was born into a world of complex, shifting forces and allegiances, both religious and political. Indeed, the situation changed so swiftly that

there is almost no resemblance between the political maps of Spain for 1000 and 1050, or again between those covering the times of the birth and death of El Cid.

For much of this time the country was in a continual state of war, with the Moors in the south and the Christians in the north constantly invading each others' borders. However, there was never any clear dividing line between north and south, neither culturally nor physically. Despite a veneer of Islamicism, many of the Spanish Moslems were originally of Gothic or Iberio–Roman stock. They were separated from their northern neighbours only by religious beliefs. Furthermore, since at this time Islam was pursuing a policy of particular openness towards other religions, less of a barrier existed than is sometimes assumed. Indeed, there was such a degree of integration between the two that even modern Spain retains a powerful element of Orientalism within its cultural makeup.

Moorish Spain came into being over a period of several hundred years – from the period of the first Moslem conquest in the eighth century, to the eventual re-conquest by Christians from the north of the peninsula in the later part of the thirteenth century. In the interim there existed a period of extraordinary cross-fertilization between Christian and Arabic cultures. In the words of the historian Pierre Vilar:

Moorish Spain was in fact a crucible in which were fused the contributions of diverse cultures . . . The products of this crucible filter across Christian Europe – scholastic philosophy, romanesque art, the school of medicine at Montpelier, the lyric poetry of the troubadours and the mystical poetry of Dante.

(*Spain: A Brief History*)

This interaction occurred because of the very fragmentation experienced by the country. After the breakdown of the Omyniad caliphates under Al-Mansur around 1030, Spain became a patchwork of small communities and states. Each claimed a king – or even, in one case, an emperor – and they included the purely Christian, the Moslem-influenced, the purely Moorish, and the Christian-influenced Islamicism. It was an extraordinarily fluid ratio of exchange which would be hard to parallel today. Perhaps a graphic parallel would be to imagine that a country existed in the middle of Europe which was at one and the same time Catholic, Protestant, Jewish and Islamic, while sharing equally the cultural and economic influence of the USA, USSR, and China!

At this time, the Christian factions within the Caliphates (ex-slaves and captives who had risen to high office under Al-Mansur) requested help from the Court of Castile. This was an extraordinary state of affairs but one which enabled Rodrigo del Bivar to serve so many masters without apparent conflict. It is also the reason why he could lay claim to a rich blend of cultures, having an excellent grasp of the European legal system and Arabic poetry and customs. This was reflected too in dress that combined Moorish robes with European mail and weaponry.

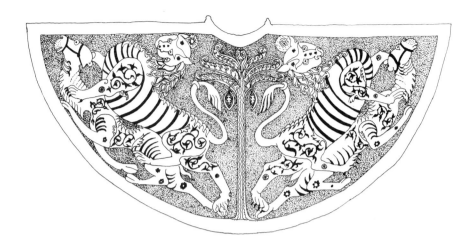

The length of time during which the frontiers of the Christian and Moorish regions continued to shift, meant that there was ample opportunity for cultural and religious exchange. There seems to have existed a form of Spanish Islam which was like nothing then available anywhere in Europe. When they were not fighting each other, the kings and caliphs were just as likely to be seeking each other's protection or vasalage. Thus, while these enlightened times continued, there existed little of the prejudice and fanaticism which were engendered by the Crusades.

Mix of Cultures

The cultural achievements of the Moors in Spain far outstripped those of the semi-barbarian north. Philosophy, medicine and the arts flourished in an enlightened atmosphere which existed scarcely anywhere else at the time. Moktadir and Mutamin, two of the Moslem lords with whom El Cid took service during his years of exile, were themselves scholars and poets of no small skill. Rodrigo must have learned a great deal from these intelligent, cultured people. Certainly his years with the Moors seem to have changed him, softening without blunting his warlike character.

In cities such as Toledo, which was reconquered by the Christian forces in 1085, an even more extraordinary mix of philosophies and beliefs obtained in something approaching harmony. A strong Jewish faction introduced the roots of the mystical system known as Qabalism. Similarly, there were practitioners, among both Moslem and Christian, of the 'hermetic arts' of alchemy, science and mystical theology.

In the north of Spain, on the other hand, there was a dearth of learning and an almost total disregard for the arts – except where Moorish influence was most strongly felt. Philosophy was frowned upon as almost certainly heretical, while the Catholic Church generally strove to outlaw even classical learning in favour of theological treatises.

There arose therefore an interesting situation. The Christian Spanish had looked towards their Moslem neighbours as arbiters of culture and learning. Yet, when faced once again with war between north and south, Christian and Moor, they found themselves unable to relate to their brothers in France or Italy, who in turn regarded them as scandalously Islamicised. As Ramon Pidal puts it:

By the eleventh century, Al Andalus was populated by an extremely heterogeneous mass, part of which was still Christian whilst another part was only half Moslem.

Political maps of the time show how complex the situation really was when Rodrigo began to exercise an influence. From the eighth century onward, there was a strong Christian presence in the northerly mountainous regions of Asturias, Cantabria and Galicia; while in the south the caliphates flourished in Cordoba, Seville, Toledo and Granada. Between these two, an unequivocal dividing line made the plateaux of Leon and Burgos a kind of no-mans-land, across which the two forces ranged more or less in a continual dispute until the middle of the tenth century. Then the forces of the Asturian kings pushed further south, founding states in Leon, Castile and Burgos. It is the fates of these kingdoms which form the background of El Cid's area of greatest activity. Had he never existed, it is probable that the Almoravid Moors, under their fanatical leader Yusuf, would have overrun a far greater area of central Spain – and perhaps prevented the gradual blurring of the two cultures which produced the later kingdoms of Moorish Spain and thereafter the great empire of the sixteenth century.

Arms and Battle Tactics

Two things gave the Christian forces in Spain superiority over their Moslem foes: the weight of their armour and horses, and their possession of massive siege engines. Castile itself had been named after the fortresses

The mangonel, which projected massive, damaging boulders and was a vital engine of siege warfare for the Christian forces.

58

built along the border between Christian and Moslem Spain, and essentially those who held these castles held the greatest degree of control over the lands on either side. For this reason, the great part of reports relating to warfare in this period concern sieges. We hear endlessly of Rodrigo taking various fortified cities and castles – only to lose them later and often in a matter of months.

By this time, the Christians had virtually perfected the art of siege warfare, using the powerful mangonel, among other massive siege engines. This machine could project massive boulders against the walls of a besieged castle with the power of a cannon. Similarly, the trebuchet could lob the lifeless carcass of a horse (or more often a human corpse) over the walls, to add to the disease already raging within.

The Moors depended more on starvation tactics and in sheer weight of numbers; they scarcely ever adapted to the use of siege towers or other engines of war, until the widespread use of cannon and gunpowder several centuries later.

However, on open ground, the Moors' skill as horsemen and the magnificent Arab steeds they rode, gave them a positive advantage over the heavily armoured war-horses of the Christians, which were more like carthorses, slow and heavy against the speedy, light Arab mounts.

The Moslems also wore much lighter armour and carried light swords, bows and spears. Again, these gave them the advantage when it came to the swift 'attack-and-run' tactics which they frequently employed. The heart-shaped shields of the Moslems, called *adarga*, proved so popular that they were sometimes adopted by their opponents.

The great castle of Montellana–Coronil in Seville. It saw much of the fighting between Moors and Christians during El Cid's lifetime.

59

However, in a head-on clash, the weight and armour-piercing qualities of the Christian forces were virtually unstoppable.

Nonetheless, the cost of maintaining a fully armoured force was considerable; hence the frequent failure of kings like Alfonso to raise sufficiently large forces. Weapons and armour, measured in the equivalent of cows, have been quoted as being worth as much as:

Helmet *6 cows*
Mail-coat *12 cows*
Sword and scabbard *7 cows*
Leg armour *6 cows*
Lance and shield *2 cows*
Horse *12 cows*

Both sides made use of bows, though the Moslems were by far the more proficient in their use. In hand-to-hand fighting, once again the huge and heavy broad-swords of the Christians proved superior over the light, curved scimitars of their adversaries. Again, in the use of spears, the Christian knight, crouched behind his kite-shaped shield, atop his massive war horse could topple a lightly armed man completely out of the saddle – and probably spear him through in the process.

All of these qualities, when duly accounted for, amounted to a virtual condition of stalemate between the opposing forces. The almost weekly loss and gain of territory depended entirely on the skills of leadership and prevailing conditions. In a straight fight, the Christians usually won; in skirmishes, the Moslem forces held their own and often overcame their opponents with fanatical zeal.

Moorish infantry and cavalry, armed with bows, swords and spears, and carrying small round shields.

The Courts of Leon and Castile

Ferdinand I of Castile and Leon was crowned on 21st June 1038. He was a strong and greedy monarch who pursued a course of military aggrandisement from the very beginning of his reign. He desired to subjugate the whole of Moslem Spain and to integrate this vast tract of land into his own kingdom, which would then be the single greatest state in the country. So confident was he of his success that he assumed the title

Three warriors of about 1150, wearing conical helms and long mail shirts and carrying kite-shaped shields. Armed with spears and swords they reflect the style of Rodrigo's army.

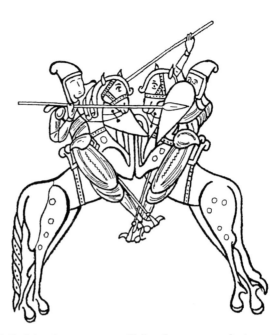

'Emperor' while his plans were still far from completion. However, his great energy and militaristic abilities enabled him to extend his sway deep into Moorish territory – in particular the Caliphate of Valencia. By 1065 he had conquered Toledo and made it a Christian–Moorish fief owing allegiance to Leon. He was on the point of taking the key fortress of Valencia in the same year, when he fell sick and died within a matter of weeks. His realm was split between his three sons Sancho, Alfonso and Garcia, along the lines of a will he had made in 1063.

To his second, favourite son Alfonso, he gave the Kingdom of Leon and the Campos Goticos, together with the tributes from the Moorish kingdom of Toledo, whose overlord he had successfully beaten into submission only a year before. To Sancho, his first-born, he gave the smaller inheritance of Castile and the tribute of Saragossa. Garcia, the third son, received Galicia and Portugal, along with the tribute of Badajar and Seville. To his daughters, Urraca and Elvira, he gave dominion over all the monasteries within his borders, on the sole understanding that they did not marry and thereby produce alternate heirs to the kingdom.

On hearing of these terms and before Ferdinand died, Sancho refused to accept this partition on the grounds that it went against the rights of the eldest son. It is said that Ferdinand made all three brothers promise to defer to Rodrigo del Bivar, putting him virtually *in loco parentis* to the *infantas*, though he was still only of an age with them.

So, with the death of Ferdinand all was quiet for a time. Sancho, ruling in Castile, at once began to extend his territories, assisted by Rodrigo, who was given the title of Ensign, a position which automatically gave him command of the army.

El Cid's Early Adventures

One of Rodrigo's earliest exploits was his win in a single combat against the champion of Navarre in order to settle a border dispute between Sancho and the Navarran king. Soon after, in 1067, he lead the armies of Castile against the Moorish city of Saragossa, subduing it effectively and extracting a firm promise of fealty and prompt payment of tribute. A Jewish chronicler attributed the success of the expedition entirely to the youthful Ensign, calling him for the first time 'Cidi', the equivalent of *Mio Cid* 'my lord'.

Then, in 1067, Ferdinand's widow died, thus removing any scruple remaining in the mind of Sancho towards honouring the partition. Within a year, Castile was at war with Leon, brother against brother. As always, Rodrigo del Bivar was in the forefront of the action.

The first action in the brief war was the battle of Llantada Plain on 19th July 1068. Castile was the victor, but instead of surrendering himself, as had previously been agreed, Alfonso fled south. Gathering his forces, he attacked the Moorish state of Badajoz, evincing a still higher tribute than was already paid to the third brother Garcia.

The result was a further outbreak of hostilities between the three sons of Ferdinand, with Sancho pretending to side with Garcia against Alfonso, while really waiting his moment to annex Galicia and Portugal.

Ramon Pidal gives a rounded portrait of the brothers at this time:

Garcia of Galicia lacked the ability possessed by his brothers and accordingly was the first victim of the discord among them all. Sancho was ambitious, headstrong, and overbearing and was noted for his indomitable courage . . . Alfonso, on the other hand, though go-ahead and energetic, was of a docile nature and readily deferred to his parents and his eldest sister Urraca, so that he became the favourite son and developed all the traits of a spoilt child.

Whether El Cid acted in a position of arbiter, as Ferdinand had intended, is not known; he seems to have stepped aside from the almost continuous wrangling of the brothers. In 1071, this conflict resulted in the capture and exile of Garcia and the subsequent division of his lands between Sancho and Alfonso. Some of the near contemporary songs which have survived from the period describe Rodrigo himself as capturing Garcia and handing him over to the brothers. It may be that he saw this as the best means of curtailing a war that was tearing apart Christian Spain.

With Garcia effectively out of the running, relations between Sancho and Alfonso worsened. Several border engagements took place, culminating in the battle of Golpejera. Here Sancho was heard to remark that he was the equal of a thousand men while Rodrigo was equal to another hundred. El Cid replied, modestly, that he was only equal to one man at a time, and that as for the rest it was up to God. However, in the battle which followed it was certainly Rodrigo who helped turn the tide of events for Sancho. Alfonso was taken prisoner, possibly by El Cid himself, and subsequently exiled to Toledo. With him went several

members of the Beni-Gomez family, and it is from this that their hatred of Rodrigo dates.

Sancho meanwhile had himself crowned king of Leon, and thus came to rule over the most extensive kingdom in the whole of Christian Spain.

However, his success was to be short-lived. His sister Urraca, who was believed to harbour an elicit passion for Alfonso, raised a rebellion against Sancho. When he arrived outside her castle of Zamora, she sent a man into the royal camp to murder him. Sancho fell dying outside his own pavilion while Rodrigo and others gave chase. However, the assassin escaped back to Zamora, which opened its gates to him.

Sancho's death at the age of 34 struck fear into the hearts of his followers, many of whom fled. Only Rodrigo was able to rally enough men to escort the King's body to its resting place in the monastery of Ona.

Urraca at once sent messengers to Alfonso who, having won the support of the Moorish king of Toledo, left his place of exile to proclaim himself King of Castile, Leon and Galicia. At the same time he proclaimed Urraca as Queen, giving her the status she would normally have attained if she were actually his consort.

But not all the lords of the kingdoms supported Alfonso. Rodrigo del Bivar was one who did not. Indeed, in a remarkable episode, El Cid is said to have forced Alfonso to swear an oath on sacred relics to the effect

El Cid leads his heavily-armed and mounted soldiers in a desperate foray from the besieged fortress of Valencia. The sheer weight and ferocity of their charge carries them through the massed ranks of their Moorish adversaries.

that he had nothing to do with his brother's murder. In this, Rodrigo once again displayed his judgement of what was best for Spain, for under this oath Alfonso gained the support of those who doubted his right to rule, as well as the support of El Cid himself, who now showed himself willing to stand by the new King.

Alfonso took the oath, but he never forgave Rodrigo for forcing him to humble himself before the rest of his vassals.

Status, Marriage and Banishment

El Cid now became an honoured member of Alfonso's court – but he no longer held the high office of Ensign as he had during Sancho's reign. Also his foes, the Beni-Gomez family, and in particular Garcia Ordonez, began a rise to power almost in equal measure to the decline of El Cid.

Meanwhile, the fate of the unfortunate Garcia was now sealed. On the advice of his sister, Alfonso summoned his youngest and only surviving brother who, expecting to be restored to his throne, came willingly. He was immediately seized and thrown into prison, where he remained in chains for a further seventeen years, finally falling sick and dying before a suddenly contrite Alfonso could order his chains removed. Garcia's epitaph, written by a monk of Leon, made clear the opinion of the time:

Here lies Garcia, King of Galicia and Portugal, taken captive by his brother's craft. He died in chains on 22nd March, 1090.

In 1074 Alfonso surprisingly arranged an excellent marriage for El Cid with his own niece Donna Ximena Diaz. By all accounts she was something of a beauty. Also, being of royal descent from the House of Aragon, her marriage not only demonstrated to all that Rodrigo stood in high favour with the King, but also helped heal the breach between Castile and Leon. Ximena was seen as representing the former, while Rodrigo, who had formally renounced his rights as a Castilian noble, now stood for Leon.

Thus, for a time, Rodrigo's fortunes were restored. But gradually the Beni-Gomez family worked on the mind of Alfonso. They reminded him of the ignominious episode of the oath-taking, and pointed out that Rodrigo now had a personal 'army' almost as large as the King's. Matters came to a head when Rodrigo lead his men against a revolt of both Christians and Moors at Toledo, a revolt in which the Beni–Gomez family were certainly involved. Diego Ordonez lost no time in accusing El Cid of seeking to further his own ends by laying claim to Toledo, something which Rodrigo never appears to have intended.

The outcome was that Alfonso banished his most trusted vassal, giving him ten days to leave Castile and Leon.

Bestowing his wife and children in the safety of the monastery at Cardena, Rodrigo departed to his exile. However, his departure was more like triumph since he took with him some 2000 men who preferred

El Cid upholds his honour and that of his King by defeating an enemy champion in single combat. Having unhorsed each other, the two men finish the fight on foot, in a hand-to-hand trial of strength.

to go into exile with him rather than remain in Alfonso's service. The next few years were to establish Rodrigo as one of the truly remarkable soldiers of his time. They were to be wandering years, but they were to end in triumph.

Exile and the Peril out of Africa

The normal recourse of exiled Spanish knights was to the nearest Moorish court, but Rodrigo made instead for the Kingdom of Barcelona. There he attempted to persuade the counts Ramon and Berenguer to aid him in taking Saragossa, a key fortress which King Ferdinand had long sought to bring under his sway.

Rodrigo met with a cold and scornful reception from the counts, who believed they had no need of a renegade knight with a rather large force of his own. So he took an extraordinary step, going directly to Moktadir, the Moslem ruler of Saragossa, and pledging his sword and men to the Moorish prince. Moktadir, who was seriously threatened by the neighbouring kingdoms of Navarre and Aragon, gladly accepted. When he died shortly after the arrival of El Cid, his son Motamid ratified the agreement and honoured Rodrigo by placing him in joint command of the army.

Rodrigo and Motamid rapidly began to make inroads into the border territory separating the Caliphates of Saragossa and Lerida. The latter was in the hands of Motamid's younger brother, who at once made an alliance with most of the states of Catalonia, including Barcelona, where El Cid had recently offered his services and been turned away.

It was the same story over again, brother against brother, neighbour against neighbour; and as before Rodrigo was caught in the middle. Nevertheless, he quickly captured Count Berenger and slaughtered most of his followers when he overwhelmed their camp outside the city of Tamarinte. Upon his return to Saragossa, El Cid was treated as a hero in exactly the same way as if he had been a Moslem. Motamid heaped gifts upon him, gold and jewels and rich silks. But Rodrigo was not like other mercenaries; he made it clear that he required nothing for himself. Instead, he negotiated an unofficial treaty which made Saragossa subject to Castile and Leon, and established the Caliphate as a virtual protectorate of Alfonso's kingdom.

There then followed an episode which further proved Cid's loyalty and Alfonso's treacherous nature. The Emperor – as he was by then styling himself – led an attack on a castle close to the border of Saragossa. In the event, he was defeated and fled after the death of most of his forces. Rodrigo, hearing of this, rushed to Alfonso's aid and for a moment it seemed that the Emperor would relent and rescind El Cid's banishment.

However, though Rodrigo was willing to give up his exalted position at Saragossa, Alfonso regained his nerve and at once again turned against his ally – and El Cid returned to Saragossa.

Alfonso entered a period of personal success which nearly eclipsed El Cid for some two years. Then, in the winter of 1085, Alfonso arrived at the gates of Saragossa and laid siege to the city. Rodrigo, who was elsewhere at the time, heard the news with dismay. His honour would not permit him to attack his sovereign, yet he still owed allegiance to Motamid.

He chose to do nothing, and for a time remained in a distant castle as a virtual prisoner of conscience.

Alfonso pressed forward on all fronts. After a heavy assault, he took the great city of Toledo which became his chief fortress on the eastern frontier, extending his kingdom still further into Moorish territory. Many of the Moslem kings now came forward with tributes and it seemed, briefly, that most of Moorish Spain was about to fall to the Christians. This would indeed have made it one of the greatest empires in Europe. But two men prevented this, one indirectly, the other by force of arms: Rodrigo del Bivar and the Almoravid chieftain, Yusuf ibn Teshufin.

The Almoravids were really Berbers from the region of the Sahara. In the eleventh century, they were one of two nomadic tribes to erupt into sudden and ferocious activity, for at the other end of the Mediterranean, the Seljuk Turks poured into Asia Minor.

The Almoravids swiftly overran much of Africa and the Sudan, restoring these countries to orthodox Islamic practice. This they administered with sword and fire, destroying taverns and burning musical instruments as symbols of moral corruption.

It was to these fanatical warriors, and above all to their chieftain, that both Motamid and the Caliph of Badajoz appealed for aid against the steady encroachments of Alfonso. Having twice refused on the grounds that he had first to win Tangier and Ceuta (which he accomplished in 1084), Yusuf finally turned his attention to Spain at Motamid's third desperate request.

He landed, with a vast army, on 30th June 1086 and was met by Motamid and the Moslem Kings of Granada and Malaga at the head of their own forces.

Alfonso, hearing the news, at once raised the siege of Saragossa and began to assemble his own forces. The two armies met at Sagrajas and the first to engage with the Christians were Motamid's own native Spanish Moslems. Yusuf held back, coolly remarking that both sides were their enemies and that the more they slaughtered each other the better.

Finally, Yusuf advanced and the thunderous roll of the Moorish

The royal bodyguard of King Alfonso III (866–909) armed with swords, lances and shields, both round and kite-shaped.

drums was heard for the first time on Spanish soil. The compact, organized attack of the Moors shook the Christians; they were more used to single combats where the actions of one man could turn the day. The disciplined ranks of the Almoravid army inflicted terrible losses. They were more lightly armed than Alfonso's knights, but their new way of fighting turned the scales in their favour.

Finally, Yusuf led into the fray his own Black Guards, consisting of 4000 men. Armed with light Indian swords and shields of hippopotamus hide, they fought their way through to the King, forcing him to withdraw, wounded in the thigh.

At the end of the day, Alfonso escaped with barely 500 men, most of whom were wounded. Meanwhile Yusuf caused the heads of the slain to be cut off and piled in heaps, from the top of which his muezzins called the faithful to prayer.

Now, at last, Alfonso called out to El Cid to come to his aid. He sent waggon-loads of treasure and a great entourage of knights to Saragossa with requests for a formal reconciliation. In effect, he need not have bothered; he had only to ask in the name of Spain and Rodrigo would have come.

The two men met in Toledo in the spring of 1087 and with the exception of El Cid's old enemies, there was general rejoicing from those who believed that if Rodrigo had commanded the army at Sagrajas the outcome would have been different.

Yusuf, meanwhile, much to everyone's astonishment, returned to Africa, having learned of the death of his son. He left only a token force of 3000 horsemen under the command of Motamid.

Spanish Christendom thus enjoyed a respite and Alfonso lost no time in consolidating his battered forces. The losses at the Battle of Sagrajas had been great and not even the addition of El Cid's men could make it anything like as strong as it had been before the coming of Yusuf.

However, Rodrigo was disinclined to sit behind the walls of Saragossa. He set about raising an army of his own to win back the lands lost in the recent campaign. Many men, elated at the prospect of fighting under El Cid, flocked to him.

With a force totalling some 7000, he began to subdue much of eastern Castile, making it as strong as it had been before Sagrajas. He also succeeded in winning pledges from the rulers of Valencia, then perhaps the most prized city of Spain.

This astonishing success, considering the size of his forces and the difficulty of much of the terrain over which he fought, only succeeded in outraging Alfonso, who seems to have believed – or been persuaded to believe – that El Cid intended to set up a rival kingdom in Valencia. However, before the King's unjust rage had time to ripen, news came that Yusuf had returned and was marching north. Alfonso at once set out to meet him, sending a peremptory command to Rodrigo to join him.

Somehow, in the confusion of rapid troop movements, El Cid never succeeded in joining with the royal army, though he certainly attempted to do so. Yusuf, who had returned with a smaller force than before and doubted the strength of his Spanish allies, abruptly withdrew. Alfonso was victorious without striking a blow; and his anger at the failure of El Cid to join him knew no bounds. Egged on by Rodrigo's old enemies, the Ordonez, he again pronounced a judgement of exile – this time backing it up by confiscating all El Cid's lands and goods. He even went so far as to imprison Rodrigo's wife Ximena, and his children; and though he soon released them he refused to listen to El Cid's demand to settle his innocence by right of combat. For the second time, and only two years after his triumphal return, Rodrigo was again in exile. This time he was virtually friendless, and his old comrade and employer, Motamid had died, leaving his son Mostain to rule over Saragossa. El

An eleventh-century manuscript's depiction of war between Christians and Moors, and its inevitable outcome — baptism or execution.

69

Cid's future seemed anything but happy, yet events were to take a dramatic turn in the months ahead.

The Struggle for Valencia

Exiled for the second time and without the support of many of the Castilian knights who had followed him before, Rodrigo once again displayed his qualities of a great commander. With a greatly reduced army, he marched into the kingdoms of Deria and Lerida. Capturing two strong castles, which he made his base, he secured a whole caveful of treasure belonging to the Lord of Lerida.

With this money, he was able to pay all his supporters, and with this added incentive he pressed the Moorish Caliphs so hard that they submitted to him, sueing for peace in the April of 1090. Rodrigo then advanced again on Valencia with extra forces supplied by his recent enemies of Deria.

Al-Kadir, the timid and vacillating ruler of Valencia, capitulated without delay, restoring the tribute he had been paying to El Cid before his second banishment. Rodrigo marched into Valencia in triumph, only to learn that his old adversary Berenguer of Barcelona – who had never forgiven the Cid for capturing him in an earlier campaign – had formed an alliance with the Moorish lord of Lerida and El Cid's own sometime ally Mostain of Saragossa. He also visited Alfonso and tried to enlist his support. Rather to the surprise of all, the Emperor refused. Even without him, the force against which Rodrigo now found himself ranged was vastly superior to his own. Leaving the safety of Valencia, he marched swiftly to a wooded valley near Tevar and fortified the three entrances with stout barriers.

There followed a swingeing series of letters between Rodrigo and Berenguer, in which each accused the other of treachery and cowardice. El Cid's final reply ended:

Thou twittest me with being a knave and a traitor, but then thou hast a lying tongue . . . Thou vauntest much of conquering me, but victory is in the hands of the Almighty, not in thine. Enough then of words, and let us fight it out like very knights. Come quickly and receive thy wonted reward!

(Pidal)

While this exchange was going on, Rodrigo had allowed certain of his men to desert to the other side, taking with them the story that El Cid was about to escape by night through one of the passes. This achieved the objective of making Berenguer split his force into three groups, each to watch one of the passes from the valley.

There then followed a confused series of night manoeuvres, which

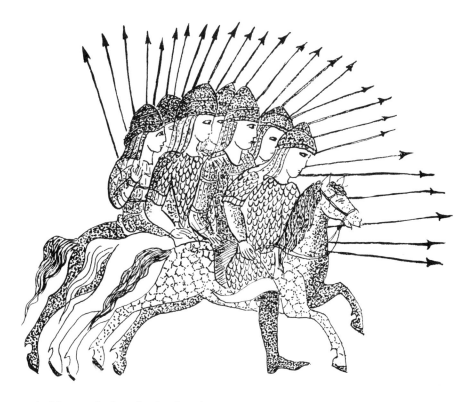

El Cid's charging cavalrymen, riding in a tightly disciplined formation, could strike at their enemy with tremendous force, wheeling and then retreating swiftly.

ended in confusion for both sides. Men from each force blundered to and fro in the darkness and El Cid himself was slightly wounded. However, his well-trained followers carried the assault without him, capturing Berenguer and 5000 of his men without any great losses of their own. The proud Count of Barcelona was thus forced to recognize the abilities of the man whose service he had once refused.

After this, most of the east and south-east of Moorish Spain offered tribute to El Cid, acknowledging him as their overlord and paying out 95,000 dinars a year for his protection.

By 1090 Rodrigo had succeeded in establishing a huge protectorate in the east which he found increasingly hard to maintain. Yusuf had returned briefly to Spanish soil, only to depart again, leaving behind a sizeable force of men. Consequently, there was a constant danger of those Moorish princes owing allegiance to El Cid calling upon him for aid, or simply reneging on their agreements and going over in force to the Almoravid leader.

This delicate balance had to be maintained. Rodrigo strove mightily not to offend his Moorish subjects, especially in Valencia which became his base of operations over the succeeding months. He ruled with justice and mercy, befriending the Moors rather than seeking to overpower them with his presence.

Such was the success of El Cid's enlightened rule that even Alfonso began to follow suit, ceasing his raids on the Andalusian Moors and seeking treaties rather than warfare. Slowly, what was beginning to emerge – largely as a result of El Cid's efforts – was a Spanish kingdom where both Christian and Moor could live at peace.

So successful was the new pattern that when Yusuf made a third entry into Spain in 1090, he met with absolutely no support from the Caliphs; they either ignored him or actually placed obstacles in his path. The Almoravid chieftain's desire was to reconquer Toledo. He failed in this and retired, as Ramon Pidal puts it, 'completely baffled', leaving Alfonso and El Cid in a position of even greater strength.

The King now prepared to mount an attack on Granada and, thanks to the request of his queen in a personal letter to Rodrigo, El Cid joined him, raising the siege of Leira just as the city was about to capitulate rather than fail Alfonso.

But once again, El Cid's loyalty proved insufficient to satisfy the King. Although the two men rode together to Granada, Rodrigo made the mistake of pitching his tents closer than Alfonso's to the walls of the city. In this he was probably hoping to answer those who had claimed that fear was the cause of his failure to appear during the campaign at Valencia. Alfonso chose to see this as a further sign of Rodrigo's pride; once again the two men parted without reconciliation.

The brief moment of semi-unity in Spain was over almost before it had begun. Yusuf's forces returned in strength and began to win back many of the states so recently conquered by Alfonso and by El Cid in their separate campaigns. Within two years, all trace of Alfonso's Moorish protectorate in Granada and Andalusia had vanished. The Almoravids held the south firmly. Only Rodrigo now stood between them and prevented the whole of Moslem Spain from reverting to independent Moorish rule.

From Valencia, El Cid began to show his true strength, gradually extending his sway until he was virtual ruler of the great part of eastern Spain. At forty-five years of age he was at the height of his powers, determined to drive out the Almoravids and bring about a united Spain. To this end, he began to negotiate with other Christian princes. Unlike Alfonso, they chose to recognize his worth and to aid him in the war against the African Moors.

Knowing that the more treaties he himself signed, the greater would be the King's suspicion, Rodrigo did his utmost to bring about peace between Moslem lords and Christian princes.

Initially, Alfonso tried to frustrate his plans, but after El Cid had firmly put an end to the power of his old enemy Garcia Ordonez, the King gave way and finally revoked El Cid's exile.

Rodrigo now stood solidly as a unique power in the east. Valencia, over which he was only nominal ruler, became virtually a kingdom with El Cid as its Lord. His deeds had made his name synonymous with victory; the Almoravids feared and hated him; he had overcome all his

enemies and won his way back to the position of Alfonso's vassal – although, in fact, he overshadowed the King in such a way that Alfonso virtually faded from the scene in the next few years. It was Rodrigo's actions that now stood out in the notice of the people: it was El Cid's name they called in the streets.

In the middle of the year 1092, Rodrigo journeyed to Saragossa, where he received a friendly welcome from Mostain, and began to prepare his assault on the Almoravids in the south of the country. He was away from Valencia for a total of nine months and in that time two dramatic events took place. Yusuf sent a large force into Valencia and every fortress along the road to the city surrendered without a fight. When the Almoravid general sent a token force of twenty mounted warriors to the gates of the

Castle of Sadaba, Saragossa, and one of El Cid's strongholds from which he rode forth to attack the Moorish cities and castles.

73

city, their arrival caused such consternation that it was believed that there were actually 500 or more. Panic spread through the city, followed by rebellion in the royal palace. The ageing king, Al-Kadir, was murdered and one of his viziers proclaimed the new overlord.

When news of this reached El Cid, he at once set out for his city but already in a matter of ten days, much of what he had achieved was undone. Granada, Seville, Malaga, Almeria, Murcia and Deria all fell to Yusuf's triumphant hoard. Rodrigo raised his standard at Juballa, a strong castle on the borders of Valencia, and from there began to raise an army to reconquer the city which had so recently been under his command. He sent a letter demanding its surrender, but its new ruler replied that the mighty Yusuf was near at hand and that if El Cid wished, he, the ruler of Valencia, would use his influence to gain El Cid a position under the true ruler of Spain!

Rodrigo now began a systematic war of attrition, biting deep into Valencian territory and reducing several of its castles to rubble. He also raided the villages around the city itself, carrying off cattle and prisoners. A poor response from Valencia was easily overcome and within the city there was much murmuring against the new ruler.

Within a month, Valencia was virtually an island in the middle of El Cid's forces; by July they were ready to sue for peace, which Rodrigo granted, on condition that all Almoravid soldiers left immediately.

With this achieved and with Rodrigo again in command of Valencia, the cards were dealt for the last hand between the Champion of Spain and the wily Moorish Emir. Yusuf had written demanding that El Cid leave Valencia at once. Rodrigo replied, in a letter which was sent to all the Moslem rulers, implying that Yusuf did not dare to cross the sea and face him.

In fact, it was to be another two years before the situation changed radically. In that time, there were frequent skirmishes between the Christians and Almoravids, and Valencia several times closed its gates to El Cid while he was engaged in campaigning in other parts of the country. Finally, on 15th June 1094, the city gave itself up totally to Rodrigo after a siege that had lasted nineteen months. This time, there was no question of nominal suzerainty: El Cid was virtually King of Valencia, though uncrowned. He sent for his wife and their three children, who took up residence with him in the old palace.

Now, Christian knights from all over Spain began to flock to his banner. Soon El Cid was able to count upon a force of some 8000 Christians and three times that number of Moslem warriors, both from Valencia itself and from Saragossa, Tortossa and Albarracin.

But Yusuf could no longer allow the continuance of El Cid's foothold in the east. He therefore despatched a force of some 150,000 horse and 3000 foot soldiers under the generalship of his nephew Mohammed, with orders to crush the power of the Campeador for ever.

Vengeance and Death

The battle of Cuarte took place near Valencia in December 1094. Here, the Christian forces defeated the Almoravids resoundingly, killing and driving off literally thousands of the Moors. El Cid himself fought like ten men and when he returned to the city he was bloody but victorious. He had used new tactics against the Moors, riding out suddenly at the head of a force of heavily armoured and mounted knights. They cut a swathe through the massed black–clad warriors, and then turning swiftly trampled back over their disorganized ranks. Legend has it that it was here that Yusuf met his death beneath the hooves of his enemies' steeds; here also that El Cid received a fatal wound. In reality, Yusuf was not even present and El Cid was to live for several more years.

The *Poema del Cid* describes his return to Valencia, where he was greeted by Ximena and their daughters:

> *See the bloody sword and sweating steed;*
> *thus are Moors vanquished on the field.*

The booty from the battle was tremendous. Rodrigo himself acquired 1000 horses, and he sent 200 of these to Alfonso along with the elaborate silken tent of the Almoravid leader, its carved posts decorated with gold.

Battle between two opposing groups of eleventh-century knights. Note the small round shields and long mail coats.

75

So complete was this victory that it ensured a kind of uneasy peace for nearly three years. Then, in 1097, Yusuf returned to Spain once more. In the fighting which ensued, Rodrigo's son Diego was slain, fighting alongside Alfonso, El Cid having remained in Valencia waiting for an attack which never came.

So great was Rodrigo's grief that he was almost paralysed for several weeks. Not only was the death of Diego the cause of personal sorrow, it also spelled the end of his family line.

Now aged fifty-four years, Rodrigo was still a splendid figure, possessed of as much energy and strength as in his youth – but he had campaigned almost unceasingly for nearly thirty years against the Moors and against Christian enemies. He had been wounded several times, twice seriously enough to have his life despaired of; he had twice suffered the rigours of exile. All this had taken its toll and there was no opportunity to rest or recover from either private loss or public defeat.

Gathering a new army, El Cid advanced on the Moorish forces, then holding the Castle of Murviedo in some strength. He laid siege to the fortress and gradually weakened it to the point of collapse. But the siege was to drag on into the summer of 1098 before the fortress finally capitulated and Rodrigo was able to enter in triumph and order Mass to be sung in one of the main squares.

With this, El Cid at once avenged the death of his son and once again showed that any attempt to reconquer Valencia was fruitless while he still lived. But the long-expected battle between the Campeador and the Emir was not to be. By now in his eighties, Yusuf would never again return to Spain – he too had been worn down by long years of struggle to remove the thorn of El Cid from his side. At best, he would now only send fresh generals against the Christian force; but even after El Cid's death, much of the heart had gone out of the Moorish invaders.

Rodrigo died suddenly at Valencia on Sunday, 10th July, 1099. He was fifty-five and still filled with plans for a united Spain. Ximena, who survived him by fifteen years, held Valencia for only a short time. It was only a matter of months before she was forced to withdraw even with the support of Alfonso (who now that the Cid was dead finally recognized the worth of his finest knight). Valencia returned to Moslem rule, along with the majority of the lands won back by Rodrigo's efforts.

Alfonso himself did not die until 1134 but, without the power of El Cid's support, he made no further inroads against the Moors.

But the idea of a united Spain did not completely die with El Cid. In time, the borders between Christian and Moslem grew more blurred, though there were many bloody wars still to be fought. During that time Spain became a cultural bridgehead between east and west. El Cid's remarkable achievements were recorded in poem and song, and grew with the telling until he became Spain's national hero. It is to the history of some of these works that one must turn for the last part of the story.

Poema del Cid and its Sources

Only eleven years after El Cid's death, a Moorish historian named Ibn Alcama wrote an account of the fall of Valencia, which he had witnessed, under the title *Eloquent Evidence of the Great Calamity*. He blamed the fall of the city on the impiety and general degeneracy of the people, who had

Monument to El Cid Campeador at Burgos, near which he was born.

been so foolish as to ally themselves with Christians in the first place. Not surprisingly, he spent a considerable amount of space vilifying the enemies of Islam.

As one would expect, this work, together with one by the Portuguese Moor Ibn Bassam, is virulently opposed to El Cid. Nevertheless, it is to these two writers that we owe almost all that we know of El Cid's life from those who were his contemporaries. They enable us to see how much of the *Poema* is romantic decoration (actually very little) and to fit the high points of the story into the larger context of medieval Spain.

The only near contemporary Christian account, the anonymous *Historia Roderici* (of about 1110) is only concerned with two aspects of El Cid's life – his heroism and his unfailing loyalty towards Alfonso. All episodes which do not illustrate these two Christian virtues are omitted, giving only a biased, pietistic portrait of an idealized figure.

Next comes a fragmentary Latin poem known as the *Carmen*, which deals with the struggle between El Cid and the counts of Barcelona. Then, some forty years after Rodrigo's death, comes the *Poema del Cid*, one of the truly great works of medieval literature and the work from which the exploits of El Cid are generally known. It exists as a single manuscript, probably dating from 1245. It shows strong stylistic similarities to other medieval romances, in particular the *Chansons de Geste* of Charlemagne and the *Song of Roland*.

Although the emphasis of the *Poema* is on the heroic qualities of El Cid, we have a more fully rounded portrait of his life, marriage, family and exile. Also included are episodes which show Rodrigo in a less than heroic light. He is described as playing tricks on Jewish moneylenders in order to finance his soldiery, and generally behaving in a manner very far from what one might expect from the deeds of similar heroes such as Roland, Ogier or Lancelot.

Not that the anonymous author of the *Poema* ever criticizes his hero – the whole work shines with an almost feverish air of hero-worship. Rodrigo is always 'my Cid', as though the writer felt a degree of affection for his hero beyond that of author and subject. Indeed, the possibility that he may actually have known Rodrigo cannot be ruled out, and offers a tantalizing possibility that we may be reading a first-hand account.

After the *Poema* there were to be no more serious attempts to re-tell the life of El Cid with any fidelity to actual events. King Alfonso X 'the Wise', commissioned a vast chronicle of Spanish history, the *Primeva Cronica General de Espana* (c. 1289). It was written not in Latin, but in the Romance language. This drew not only on *bona fide* sources, but upon poetry, ballads and pseudo-history.

Once again, as with heroes such as Arthur, Charlemagne and Macbeth, an original core of genuine history gathered about it a coating of myth and legend which distorted the truth and added extensively to the apocryphal side of Rodrigo's life.

This set the pattern for all later accounts of El Cid up to the seventeenth century, when medieval sources were frequently questioned as to their ultimate accuracy.

From this point onwards, attitudes to El Cid were divided. They included, on the one hand, the eulogistic writings of the nineteenth century Swiss historian Johann Muller, who wrote that:

All that godliness, honour and love could make of a knight was combined in Don Rodrigo . . . This remarkable man is one of the few who . . . have been, in their own lifetime, their country's pride

(trans: Sunderland.)

But, on the other hand, they ranged to the equally fervent, though dissatisfied Masden, the Jesuit who described the earlier works as catalogues of the 'perfidy, perjury and brazen deeds of Rodrigo Diaz.' (Sunderland, after Pidal.)

After this, the figure of El Cid entered a dark period in which historian after historian, following a 1849 work of the Dutch orientalist R. Dozy, contrived to portray Rodrigo as a cruel, treacherous and often barbarian character.

Assyrian soldiers at the seige of Jerusalem in 1099. Their armour and weapons reflect perfectly the influence of both Christian and Moorish arms. Warriors who fought with El Cid would have employed such an amalgam of both kinds of weaponry.

Not until the enlightened work of Ramon Menendez Pidal in the first half of the twentieth century, was the figure of El Cid re-established in something like a clear light. Any writer dealing with Rodrigo must turn to Pidal, and this present work could certainly not have been accomplished without his scrupulous and immensely detailed account of the life and period of El Cid.

The memory of the heroism and sterling qualities of Rodrigo del Bivar have thus been enshrined for all time; his statue stands today in the main square of Burgos, staring out forever across the lands he fought so long to transform.

He was a hero of the old style, whose life and deeds left their mark on the tide of human history and became the inspiration of a whole nation.

The Life and Deeds of El Cid Campeador

The following extracts are from the earliest translation of the story of El Cid. Robert Southey (1774–1843) who was later to become poet laureate, discovered the medieval *Chronica del Cid* during his childhood in Spain, and later made a translation which became something of a best-seller in the nineteenth century. The story it tells is close to the historical details already described, but there is an overlay of romanticism which brings the dry facts to life. This selection also includes several episodes not dealt with in the first half of this book, but which are an integral part of El Cid's legend. They are arranged to make a more or less connected narrative, and, taken within the larger historical framework already described, form a more detailed story of El Cid.

The headings of the sections and the linking passages were created especially for inclusion in this selection, but the spellings and names are those used in the original extracts.

The Rise of Rodrigo del Bivar

King Don Ferdinand succeeded to the states of Castille after the death of his father King Don Sancho el Mayor, in the era 1072, which was the year of the Incarnation 1034, and from the coming of the Patriarch Tubal to settle in Spain 3197, and from the general deluge 3339, and from the creation of the world 4995, according to the computation of the Hebrews, and from the beginning of the false sect of the Moors 413. And in the year 1037 Ferdinand slew Bermudo the King of Leon in battle, who was his wife's brother, and conquered his kingdom, and succeeded to it in right of his wife Doña Sancha. So he was the first person who united the states of Castille and Leon, and the first who was called King of

Having defeated a large Christian force, the Moorish Emir Yusuf orders the heads of his foes cut off and piled in mounds. From the top of one of these, a muezzin calls the faithful to prayer.

Castille; for till this time the lords of that country had been called Counts. He was a good king, and one who judged justly and feared God, and was bold in all his doings. Before he reigned he had, by Doña Sancha his wife the Infanta Doña Urraca, his eldest daughter, who was a right excellent lady, and after her he had the Infante Don Sancho, his eldest son and heir; and then the Infanta Doña Elvira, whom after the death of the King her father, her brother King Don Alfonso married to the Count Don Garcia de Cabra. And after he became King he had the Infante Don Alfonso, and the Infante Don Garcia, who was the youngest of all. And he put his sons to read, that they might be of the better understanding, and he made them take arms, and be shown how to demean themselves in battle, and to be huntsmen. And he ordered that his daughters should be brought up in the studies beseeming dames.

In those days arose Rodrigo of Bivar, who was a youth strong in arms and of good customs; and the people rejoiced in him, for he bestirred himself to protect the land from the Moors.

At this time it came to pass that there was strife between Count Don Gomez the Lord of Gormaz, and Diego Laynez the father of Rodrigo; and the Count insulted Diego and gave him a blow. Now Diego was a man in years, and his strength had passed from him, so that he could not take vengeance, and he retired to his home to dwell there in solitude and lament over his dishonour. And he took no pleasure in his food, neither could he sleep by night, nor would he lift up his eyes from the ground, nor stir out of his house, nor commune with his friends, but turned from them in silence as if the breath of his shame would taint them. Rodrigo was yet but a youth, and the Count was a mighty man in arms, one who gave his voice first in the Cortes, and was held to be the best in the war, and so powerful that he had a thousand friends among the mountains. Howbeit all these things appeared as nothing to Rodrigo when he thought of the wrong done to his father, the first which had ever been offered to the blood of Layn Calvo. He asked nothing but justice of Heaven, and of man he asked only a fair field; and his father seeing of how good heart he was, gave him his sword and his blessing. The sword had been the sword of Mudarra in former times, and when Rodrigo held its cross in his hand, he thought within himself that his arm was not weaker than Mudarra's. And he went out and defied the Count and slew him, and smote off his head and carried it home to his father. The old man was sitting at table, the food lying before him untasted, when Rodrigo returned, and pointing to the head which hung from the horse's collar, dropping blood, he bade him look up, for there was the herb which should restore to him his appetite. The tongue, quoth he, which insulted you is no longer a tongue, and the hand which wronged you is no longer a hand. And the old man arose and embraced his son and placed him above him at the table, saying, that he who had brought home that head should be the head of the house of Layn Calvo.

In the Great Hall of Burgos, El Cid forces the treacherous King Alfonso to swear an oath on sacred relics that he had no part in his own brother's death. Alfonso is thus humbled and perjured before his nobles.

After this Diego being full of years fell asleep and was gathered to his fathers. And the Moors entered Castille, in great power, for there came with them five Kings, and they past above Burgos, and crost the mountains of Oca, and plundered Carrion, and Vilforado, and Saint Domingo de la Calzada, and Logroño, and Najara, and all that land; and they carried away many captives both male and female, and brood mares, and flocks of all kinds. But as they were returning with all speed, Rodrigo of Bivar raised the country, and came up with them in the mountains of Oca, and fell upon them and discomfited them, and won back all their booty, and took all the five Kings prisoners. Then he went back to his mother, taking the Kings with him, and there he divided the whole spoil with the hidalgos and his other companions, both the Moorish captives and all the spoil of whatever kind, so that they departed right joyfully, being well pleased with what he had done. And he gave thanks to God for the grace which had been vouchsafed to him, and said to his mother, that he did not think it good to keep the Kings in captivity, but to let them go freely; and he set them at liberty and bade them depart. So they returned each to his own country, blessing him for their deliverance, and magnifying his great bounty; and forthwith they sent him tribute and acknowledged themselves to be his vassals.

King Don Ferdinand was going through Leon, putting the Kingdom in order, when tidings reached him of the good speed which Rodrigo had had against the Moors. And at the same time there came before him Ximena Gomez, the daughter of the Count, who fell on her knees before him and said, Sir, I am the daughter of Count Don Gomez of Gormaz, and Rodrigo of Bivar has slain the Count my father, and of three daughters whom he has left I am the youngest. And, Sir, I come to crave of you a boon, that you will give me Rodrigo of Bivar to be my husband, with whom I shall hold myself well married, and greatly honoured; for certain I am that his possessions will one day be greater than those of any man in your dominions. Certes, Sir, it behoves you to do this, because it is for God's service, and because I may pardon Rodrigo with a good will. The King held it good to accomplish her desire; and forthwith ordered letters to be drawn up to Rodrigo of Bivar, wherein he enjoined and commanded him that he should come incontinently to Valencia, for he had much to communicate to him, upon an affair which was greatly to God's service, and his own welfare and great honour.

When Rodrigo saw the letters of his Lord the King, he greatly rejoiced in them, and said to the messengers that he would fulfil the King's pleasure, and go incontinently to his command. And he dight himself full gallantly and well, and took with him many knights, both his own and of his kindred and of his friends, and he took also many new arms, and came to Valencia to the King with two hundred of his peers in arms, in festival guise; and the King went out to meet him, and received him right well, and did him honour; and at this were all the Counts displeased. And when the King thought it a fit season, he spake to him and said, that Doña Ximena Gomez, the daughter of the Count whom he had slain, had come to ask him for her husband, and would forgive him her father's death; wherefore he besought him to think it good to take her to be his wife, in which case he would show him great favour. When Rodrigo heard this it pleased him well, and he said to the King that he would do his bidding in this, and in all other things which he might command; and the King thanked him much. And he sent for the Bishop of Valencia, and took their vows and made them plight themselves each to the other according as the law directs. And when they were espoused the King did them great honour, and gave them many noble gifts, and added to Rodrigo's lands more than he had till then possessed: and he loved him greatly in his heart, because he saw that he was obedient to his commands, and for all that he had heard him say.

So Rodrigo departed from the King, and took his spouse with him to the house of his mother, and gave her to his mother's keeping. And forthwith he made a vow in her hands that he would never accompany with her, neither in the desert nor in the inhabited place, till he had won five battles in the field. And he besought his mother that she would love her even as she loved him himself, and that she would do good to her and show her great honour, for which he should ever serve her with the better good will. And his mother promised him so to do; and then he departed from them and went out against the frontier of the Moors.

The Cathedral of San Isidoro, Leon. Here the Spanish kings were buried.

How Rodrigo Met with a Leper

Rodrigo set out upon the road, and took with him twenty knights. And as he went he did great good, and gave alms, feeding the poor and needy. And upon the way they found a leper, struggling in a quagmire, who cried out to them with a loud voice to help him for the love of God; and when Rodrigo heard this, he alighted from his beast and helped him, and placed him upon the beast before him, and carried him with him in this manner to the inn where he took up his lodging that night. At this were his knights little pleased. And when supper was ready he bade his knights take their seats, and he took the leper by the hand, and seated him next himself, and ate with him out of the same dish. The knights were greatly offended at this foul sight, insomuch that they rose up and left the chamber. But Rodrigo ordered a bed to be made ready for himself and for the leper, and they twain slept together. When it was midnight and Rodrigo was fast asleep, the leper breathed against him between his shoulders, and that breath was so strong that it passed through him, even through his breast; and he awoke, being astounded, and felt for the leper by him, and found him not; and he began to call him, but there was no reply. Then he arose in fear, and called for light, and it was brought him; and he looked for the leper and could see nothing; so he returned into the bed, leaving the light burning. And he began to think within himself what had happened, and of that breath which had passed through him, and how the leper was not there. After a while, as he was thus musing, there appeared before him one in white garments, who said unto him, Sleepest thou or wakest thou, Rodrigo? and he answered and said, I do not sleep: but who art thou that bringest with thee such brightness and so sweet an odour? Then said he, I am Saint Lazarus, and know that I was the leper to whom thou didst so much good and so great honour for the love of God; and because thou didst this for his sake hath God now granted thee a great gift; for whensoever that breath which thou hast felt shall come upon thee whatever thing thou desires to do, and shalt then begin, that shalt thou accomplish to thy heart's desire, whether it be in battle or aught else, so thy honour shall go on increasing from day to day; and thou shalt be feared both by Moors and Christians, and thy enemies shall never prevail against thee, and thou shalt die an honourable death in thine own house, and in thy renown, for God hath blessed thee; – therefore go thou on, and evermore persevere in doing good; and with that he disappeared.

How El Cid was Exiled

[Now] . . . King Don Alfonso assembled together all his power and went against the Moors. And the Cid should have gone with him, but he fell sick and perforce therefore abode at home. And while the King was going through Andalusia, having the land at his mercy, a great power of the Moors assembled together on the other side, and entered the land,

and besieged the castle of Gormaz, and did much evil. At this time the Cid was gathering strength; and when he heard that the Moors were in the country, laying waste before them, he gathered together what force he could, and went after them; and the Moors, when they heard this, dared not abide his coming, but began to fly. And the Cid followed them to Atienza, and to Ciguenza, and Fita, and Guadalajara, and through the whole land of St. Esteban, as far as Toledo, slaying and burning, and plundering and destroying, and laying hands on all whom he found, so that he brought back seven thousand prisoners, men and women; and he and all his people returned rich and with great honour. But when the King of Toledo heard of the hurt which he had received at the hands of the Cid, he sent to King Don Alfonso to complain thereof, and the King was greatly troubled. And then the Ricos-omes who wished ill to the Cid, had the way open to do him evil with the King, and they said to the King, Sir Ruydiez hath broken your faith, and the oath and promise which you made to the King of Toledo: and he hath done this for no other reason but that the Moors of Toledo may fall upon us here, and slay both you and us. And the King believed what they said, and was wroth against the Cid, having no love towards him because of the oath which he had pressed upon him at Burgos concerning the death of King Don Sancho his brother. And he went with all speed to Burgos, and sent from thence to bid the Cid come unto him.

Now my Cid knew the evil disposition of the King towards him, and when he received his bidding, he made answer that he would meet him between Burgos and Bivar. And the King went out from Burgos and came nigh unto Bivar; and the Cid came up to him and would have kissed his hand, but the King withheld it, and said angrily unto him, Ruydiez, quit my land. Then the Cid clapt spurs to the mule upon which he rode, and vaulted into a piece of ground which was his own inheritance, and answered, Sir, I am not in your land, but in my own. And the King replied full wrathfully, Go out of my kingdoms without any delay. And the Cid made answer, Give me then thirty days time, as is the right of the hidalgos; and the King said he would come and look for him. The Counts were well pleased at this; but all the people of the land were sorrowful. And then the King and the Cid parted. And the Cid sent for all his friends and his kinsmen and vassals, and told them how King Don Alfonso had banished him from the land, and asked of them who would follow him into banishment, and who would remain at home. Then Alvar Fañez, who was his cousin-german, came forward and said, Cid, we will all go with you, through desert and through peopled country, and never fail you. In your service will we spend our mules and horses, our wealth and our garments, and ever while we live be unto you loyal friends and vassals. And they all confirmed what Alvar Fañez had said; and the Cid thanked them for their love, and said that there might come a time in which he should guerdon them.

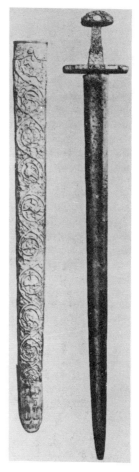

Eleventh century German sword and sheath of the type carried by Rodrigo's followers.

And as he was about to depart he looked back upon his own home, and when he saw his hall deserted, the household chests unfastened, the doors open, no cloaks hanging up, no seats in the porch, no hawks upon the perches, the tears came into his eyes, and he said, My enemies have done this . . . God be praised for all things. And he turned toward the East and knelt and said, Holy Mary Mother, and all Saints, pray to God for me, that he may give me strength to destroy all the Pagans, and to win enough from them to requite my friends therewith, and all those who follow and help me. Then he called for Alvar Fañez and said unto him, Cousin, the poor have no part in the wrong which the King hath done us; see now that no wrong be done unto them along our road: and he called for his horse. And then an old woman who was standing at her door said, Go in a lucky minute, and make spoil of whatever you wish. And with this proverb he rode on, saying, Friends, by God's good pleasure we shall return to Castille with great honour and great gain. And as they went out from Bivar they had a crow on their right hand, and when they came to Burgos they had a crow on the left.

How the Moors of Africa First Came to Spain

Now came true tidings to Valencia that the host of the Almoravides were coming, and that they were now at Lorca, and the son in law of the Miramamolin at their head, for he himself could not come, by reason that he ailed. They of Valencia took courage at these tidings, and waxed insolent, and began to devise how they should take vengeance upon Abeniaf, and upon all those who had oppressed them. And Abeniaf was in great trouble at this which was said openly concerning him, and he sent privily to the Cid, telling him to come as soon as might be. The Cid was then before Albarrazin, doing all the evil that he could, and he brake up his camp and came with his host to Juballa; and Abeniaf and the Alcaydes of Xativa and Carchayra came unto him, and they renewed their covenant to stand by each other, and be of one voice. And they took counsel and made a letter for the leader of the army of the Almoravides, wherein they told him that the Cid had made a treaty with the King of Aragon, whereby the King bound himself to help him against them; and they bade him beware how he came towards Valencia, unless he chose to do battle with eight thousand Christian horsemen, covered with iron, and the best warriors in the world. This did they thinking that he would be dismayed and turn back: but the Moor did not cease to advance, notwithstanding this letter.

How El Cid Entered Valencia

On the following day after the Christians had taken possession of the town, the Cid entered it with a great company, and he ascended the highest tower of the wall, and beheld all the city; and the Moors came unto him, and kissed his hand, saying he was welcome. And the Cid did great honour unto them. And then he gave order that all the windows of the towers which looked in upon the town should be closed up, that the Christians might not see what the Moors did in their houses; and the Moors thanked him for this greatly. And he commanded and requested the Christians that they should show great honour to the Moors, and respect them, and greet them when they met: and the Moors thanked the Cid greatly for the honour which the Christians did them, saying that they had never seen so good a man, nor one so honourable, nor one who had his people under such obedience.

And when they were all assembled, he went out unto them, to a place which was made ready with carpets and with mats, and he made them take their seats before him full honourably, and began to speak unto them, saying, I am a man who have never possessed a kingdom, neither I nor any man of my lineage. But the day when I first beheld this city I was well pleased therewith, and coveted it that I might be its Lord; and I besought the Lord our God that he would give it me. See now what his power is, for the day when I sate down before Juballa I had no more than four loaves of bread, and now by God's mercy I have won Valencia. And if I administer right and justice here God will let me enjoy it, but if I do evil, and demean myself proudly and wrongfully, I know that he will take it away. Now then let every one go to his own lands, and possess them even as he was wont to have and to hold them. He who shall find his field, or his vineyard, or his garden, desert, let him incontinently enter thereon; and he who shall find his husbanded, let him pay him that hath cultivated it the cost of his labour, and of the seed which he hath sown therein, and remain with his heritage, according to the law of the Moors. Moreover I have given order that they who collect my dues take from you no more than the tenth, because so it is appointed by the custom of the Moors, and it is what ye have been wont to pay. And I have resolved in my heart to hear your complaints two days in the week, on the Monday and the Thursday; but if causes should arise which require haste, come to me when ye will and I will give judgment, for I do not retire with women to sing and to drink, as your Lords have done, so that ye could obtain no justice, but will myself see to these things, and watch over ye as friend over his friend, and kinsman over his kinsman. And I will be Cadi and Guanzil, and when dispute happens among ye I will decide it. When he had said these things they all replied that they prayed God to preserve him through long and happy years, and four of the most honourable among them rose and kissed his hands, and the Cid bade them take their seats again.

How the Moors Attacked Valencia

The winter is past, and March is coming in. Three months Doña Ximena had been in Valencia, when tidings came to the Cid from beyond sea, that King Yucef, the son of the Miramamolin, who dwelt in Morocco,

Spanish soldier from the door of a Spanish cathedral. His shield and spear show graphically the arms carried by El Cid's armies.

was coming to lay siege unto Valencia with fifty thousand men. When the Cid heard this he gave command to store all his Castles, and had them well repaired. And he had the walls of the city prepared, and stored it well with food and with all things needful for war, and gathered together a great power of Christians and of the Moors of his seignory. Hardly had he done this before he heard that Yucef was near at hand, and coming as fast as he could come. Then the Cid assembled together the Christians in the Alcazar, and when they were assembled, he rose upon his feet and said, Friends and kinsmen and vassals, praised be God and holy Mary Mother, all the good which I have in the world I have here in Valencia; with hard labour I won the city, and hold it for my heritage, and for nothing less than death will I leave it. My daughters and my wife shall see me fight, . . . they shall see with their own eyes our manner of living in this land, and how we get our bread. We will go out against the Moors and give them battle, and God who hath thus far shown favour unto us will still continue to be our helper. When they heard this they cried out with one accord that they would do his bidding, and go out with him and fight under his banner, for certain they were that by his good fortune the Moors would be overthrown.

On the morrow the Cid took Doña Ximena by the hand, and her daughters with her, and made them go up upon the highest tower of the Alcazar, and they looked toward the sea and saw the great power of the Moors, how they came on and drew nigh, and began to pitch their tents round about Valencia, beating their tambours and with great uproar. And Ximena's heart failed her, and she asked the Cid if peradventure God would deliver him from these enemies. Fear not, honoured woman, said he; you are but lately arrived, and they come to bring you a present, which shall help marry your daughters. Fear not, for you shall see me fight by the help of God and holy Mary Mother; my heart kindles because you are here! The more Moors the more gain! The tambours sounded now with a great alarum, and the sun was shining . . . Cheer up, said my Cid; . . . this is a glorious day. But Ximena was seized with such fear as if her heart would have broken; she and her daughters had never been in such fear since the day that they were born. Then the good Cid Campeador stroked his beard and said, Fear not, all this is for your good. Before fifteen days are over, if it please God, those tambours shall be laid before you, and shall be sounded for your pleasure, and then they shall be given to the Bishop Don Hieronymo, that he may hang them up in the Church of St. Mary, Mother of God. This vow the Cid Campeador made. Now the Moors began to enter the gardens which were round about the town, and the watchman saw them and struck the bell. My Cid looked back and saw Alvar Salvadores beside him, and he said, go now, take two hundred horse, and sally upon yonder Moors who are entering the gardens; let Doña Ximena and her daughters see the good will you have to serve them. Down went Alvar Salvadores in great haste, and ordered a bell to be rung which was a signal for two hundred knights to make ready; for the history saith, that the Cid, by reason that he was alway in war, had appointed such signals for his people, that they knew when one hundred were called for, and when two, and so forth. Presently they were ready at the place of meeting, and the gate was opened which was nearest the gardens where the Moors had entered, without order; and they fell fiercely upon them, smiting and slaying. Great was the pleasure of the Cid at seeing how well they behaved themselves. And Doña Ximena and her daughters stood trembling, like women who had never seen such things before: and when the Cid saw it he made them seat themselves, so as no longer to behold it. Great liking had the Bishop Don Hieronymo to see how bravely they fought. Alvar Salvadores and his companions bestirred themselves so well that they drove the enemy to their tents, making great mortality among them, and then they turned back, whereat my Cid was well pleased; but Alvar Salvadores went on, hacking and hewing all before him, for he thought the ladies were looking on, and he pressed forward so far, that being without succour he was taken. The others returned to the city, falling back in brave order till they were out of reach of the enemy: and they had done no little in that exploit, for they slew above two hundred and fifty Moors. When my Cid saw that they who eat his bread were returned, he went down from the tower, and received them right well, and praised them for what they had done like good knights: howbeit he was full sorrowful for Alvar Salvadores that he should be in the hands of the Moors, but he trusted in God that he should deliver him on the morrow.

And the Cid assembled his chief captains and knights and people, and said unto them, Kinsmen and friends and vassals, hear me: to-day has been a good day, and to-morrow shall be a better day.

Four thousand, lacking thirty, were they who went out with my Cid, with a good will, to attack fifty thousand. They went through all the narrow places, and bad passes, and leaving the ambush on the left, struck to the right hand, so as to get the Moors between them and the town. And the Cid put his battles in good array, and bade Pero Bermudez bear his banner. When the Moors saw this they were greatly amazed; and they harnessed themselves in great haste, and came out of their tents. Then the Cid bade his banner move on, and the Bishop Don Hieronymo pricked forward with his company, and laid on with such guise, that the hosts were soon mingled together. Then might you have seen many a horse running about the field with the saddle under his belly, and many a horseman in evil plight upon the ground. Great was the smiting and slaying in short time; but by reason that the Moors were so great a number, they bore hard upon the Christians, and were in the hour of overcoming them. And the Cid began to encourage them with a loud voice, shouting God and Santiago! And Alvar Fañez at this time issued out from ambush, and fell upon them, on the side which was nearest the

Eleventh-century Norman knight with chain mail coat, kite-shaped shield, sword and long lance which could be used from horseback. With small variations, this is typical of the kind of armour worn by El Cid and his warriors.

sea; and the Moors thought that a great power had arrived to the Cid's succour, and they were dismayed, and began to fly. And the Cid and his people pursued, punishing them in a bad way. If we should wish to tell you how every one behaved himself in this battle, it is a thing which could not be done, for all did so well that no man can relate their feats. And the Cid Ruydiez did so well, and made such mortality among the Moors, that the blood ran from his wrist to his elbow! great pleasure had he in his horse Bavieca that day, to find himself so well mounted. And in the pursuit he came up to King Yucef, and smote him three times: but the King escaped from under the sword, for the horse of the Cid passed on in his course, and when he turned, the King being on a fleet horse, was far off, so that he might not be overtaken; and he got into a Castle called Guyera, for so far did the Christians pursue them, smiting and slaying, and giving them no respite, so that hardly fifteen thousand escaped of fifty that they were. And they who were in the ships, fled to Denia.

Then the Cid and his people returned to the field and began to plunder the tents. And the spoil was so great that there was no end to the riches, in gold and in silver, and in horses and arms, so that men knew not what to leave and what to take. And they found one tent which had been King Yucef's; never man saw so noble a thing as that tent was; and there were great riches therein, and there also did they find Alvar Salvadores, who had been made prisoner the yesterday, as ye have heard. Greatly did the Cid rejoice when he saw him alive and sound, and he ordered his chains to be taken off; and then he left Alvar Fañez to look to the spoil, and went into Valencia with a hundred knights. His wrinkled brow was seen, for he had taken off his helmet, and in this manner he entered, upon Bavieca, sword in hand. Great joy had Doña Ximena and her daughters, who were awaiting him, when they saw him come riding in; and he stopt when he came to them, and said, Great honour have I won for you, while you kept Valencia this day! God and the Saints have sent us goodly gain, upon your coming. Look, with a bloody sword, and a horse all sweat, this is the way that we conquer the Moors! Pray God that I may live yet awhile for your sakes, and you shall enter into great honour, and they shall kiss your hands. Then my Cid alighted when he had said this, and the ladies knelt down before him, and kissed his hand, and wished him long life. Then they entered the Palace with him, and took their seats upon the precious benches. Wife Doña Ximena, said he, these damsels who have served you so well, I will give in marriage to these my vassals, and to every one of them two hundred marks of silver, that it may be known in Castille what they have got by their services. Your daughters' marriage will come in time. And they all rose and kissed his hand; great was the joy in the Palace, it was done according as the Cid had said.

The Death of El Cid

The Cid sickened of the malady of which he died. And the day before his weakness waxed great, he ordered the gates of the town to be shut, and went to the Church of St. Peter; and there the Bishop Don Hieronymo being present, and all the clergy who were in Valencia, and the knights and honourable men and honourable dames, as many as the Church could hold, the Cid Ruydiez stood up, and made a full noble preaching, showing that no man whatsoever, however honourable or fortunate they may be in this world, can escape death; to which, said he, I am now full near; and since ye know that this body of mine hath never yet been conquered, nor put to shame, I beseech ye let not this befall it at the end, for the good fortune of man is only accomplished at his end. How this is to be done, and what ye all have to do, I will leave in the hands of the Bishop Don Hieronymo, and Alvar Fañez, and Pero Bermudez. And when he had said this he placed himself at the feet of the Bishop, and there before all the people made a general confession of all his sins, and all the faults which he had committed against our Lord Jesus Christ. And the Bishop appointed him his penance, and assoyled him of his sins. Then he arose and took leave of the people, weeping plenteously, and returned to the Alcazar, and betook himself to his bed, and never rose from it again; and every day he waxed weaker and weaker, till seven days only remained of the time appointed. Then he called for the caskets of gold in which was the balsam and the myrrh which the Soldan of Persia had sent him; and when these were put before him he bade them bring him the golden cup, of which he was wont to drink; and he took of that balsam and of that myrrh as much as a little spoon-full, and mingled it in the cup with rose-water and drank of it; and for the seven days which he lived he neither ate nor drank aught else than a little of that myrrh and balsam mingled with water. And every day after he did this, his body and his countenance appeared fairer and fresher than before, and his voice clearer, though he waxed weaker and weaker daily, so that he could not move in his bed.

On the twenty-ninth day, being the day before he departed, he called for Doña Ximena, and for the Bishop Don Hieronymo, and Don Alvar Fañez Minaya, and Pero Bermudez, and his trusty Gil Diaz; and when they were all five before him, he began to direct them what they should do after his death; and he said to them, Ye know that King Bucar will presently be here to besiege this city, with seven and and thirty Kings whom he bringeth with him, and with a mighty power of Moors. Now therefore the first thing which ye do after I have departed, wash my body with rose-water many times and well, as blessed be the name of God it is washed within and made pure of all uncleanness to receive his holy body to-morrow, which will be my last day. And when it has been well washed and made clean, ye shall dry it well, and anoint it with this myrrh and balsam, from these golden caskets, from head to foot, so that every part shall be anointed, till none be left. And you my Sister Doña Ximena, and your women, see that ye utter no cries, neither make any lamenta-

Eleventh-century Spanish soldier in mail shirt and coif, with conical helmet and long shield. The lance would have been used both to stab and as a weapon from throwing or as a lance on horseback.

tion for me, that the Moors may not know of my death. And when the day shall come in which King Bucar arrives, order all the people of Valencia to go upon the walls, and sound your trumpets and tambours, and make the greatest rejoicing that ye can. And when ye would set out for Castille, let all the people know in secret, that they make themselves ready, and take with them all that they have, so that none of the Moors in the suburb may know thereof; for certes ye cannot keep the city, neither abide therein after my death. And see ye that sumpter beasts be laden with all that there is in Valencia, so that nothing which can profit may be left. And this I leave especially to your charge, Gil Diaz. Then saddle ye my horse Bavieca, and arm him well; and ye shall apparel my body full seemlily, and place me upon the horse, and fasten and tie me thereon so that it cannot fall: and fasten my sword Tizona in my hand. And let the Bishop Don Hieronymo go on one side of me, and my trusty Gil Diaz on the other, and he shall lead my horse. You, Pero Bermudez, shall bear my banner, as you were wont to bear it; and you, Alvar Fañez, my cousin, gather your company together, and put the host in order as you are wont to do. And go ye forth and fight with King Bucar: for be ye certain and doubt not that ye shall win this battle; God hath granted me this. And when ye have won the fight, and the Moors are discomfited, ye may spoil the field at pleasure. Ye will find great riches. What ye are afterwards to do I will tell ye to-morrow, when I make my testament.

Three days after the Cid had departed King Bucar came into the port of Valencia, and landed with all his power, which was so great that there is not a man in the world who could give account of the Moors whom he brought. And there came with him thirty and six Kings, and one Moorish Queen, who was a negress, and she brought with her two hundred horsewomen, all negresses like herself, all having their hair shorn save a tuft on the top, and this was in token that they came as if upon a pilgrimage, and to obtain the remission of their sins; and they were all armed in coats of mail and with Turkish bows. King Bucar ordered his tents to be pitched round about Valencia, and Abenalfarax who wrote this history in Arabic, saith, that there were full fifteen thousand tents; and he bade that Moorish negress with her archers to take their station near the city. And on the morrow they began to attack the city, and they fought against it three days strenuously; and the Moors received great loss, for they came blindly up to the walls and were slain there. And the Christians defended themselves right well, and every time that they went upon the walls, they sounded trumpets and tambours; and made great rejoicings, as the Cid had commanded. This continued for eight days or nine, till the companions of the Cid had made ready every thing for their departure, as he had commanded. And King Bucar and his people thought that the Cid dared not come out against them, and they were the more encouraged, and began to think of making bastilles and engines wherewith to combat the city, for certes they weened that the Cid Ruydiez dared not come out against them, seeing that he tarried so long.

All this while the company of the Cid were preparing all things to go into Castille, as he had commanded before his death; and his trusty Gil Diaz did nothing else but labour at this. And the body of the Cid was prepared after this manner: first it was embalmed and anointed as the history hath already recounted, and the virtue of the balsam and myrrh was such that the flesh remained firm and fair, having its natural colour, and his countenance as it was wont to be, and the eyes open, and his long beard in order, so that there was not a man who would have thought him dead if he had seen him and not known it. And on the second day after he had departed, Gil Diaz placed the body upon a right noble saddle, and this saddle with the body upon it he put upon a frame; and he dressed the body in a *gambax* of fine sendal, next the skin. And he took two boards and fitted them to the body, one to the breast and the other to the shoulders; these were so hollowed out and fitted that they met at the sides and under the arms, and the hind one came up to the pole, and the other up to the beard; and these boards were fastened into the saddle, so that the body could not move. All this was done by the morning of the twelfth day; and all that day the people of the Cid were busied in making ready their arms, and in loading beasts with all that they had, so that they left nothing of any price in the whole city of Valencia, save only the empty houses. When it was midnight they took the body of the Cid, fastened to the saddle as it was, and placed it upon his horse Bavieca, and fastened the saddle well: and the body sate so upright and well that it seemed as if he was alive. And it had on painted hose of black and white, so cunningly painted that no man who saw them would have thought but that they were grieves and cuishes, unless he had laid his hand upon them; and they put on it a surcoat of green sendal, having his arms blazoned thereon, and a helmet of parchment, which was cunningly painted that every one might have believed it to be iron; and his shield was hung round his neck, and they placed the sword Tizona in his hand, and they raised his arm, and fastened it up so subtilly that it was a marvel to see how upright he held the sword. And the Bishop Don Hieronymo went on one side of him, and the trusty Gil Diaz on the other, and he led the horse Bavieca, as the Cid had commanded him. And when all this had been made ready, they went out from Valencia at midnight, through the gate of Roseros, which is towards Castille. Pero Bermudez went first with the banner of the Cid, and with him five hundred knights who guarded it, all well appointed. And after these came all the baggage. Then came the body of the Cid with an hundred knights, all chosen men, and behind them Doña Ximena with all her company, and six hundred knights in the rear. All these went out so silently, and with such a measured pace, that it seemed as if there were only a score. And by the time that they had all gone out it was broad day.

Twelfth-century sword, much like the weapons carried by Rodrigo and his men.

Bronze dagger of Moorish design, carved with magical symbols to protect its user from harm and to inflict the maximum damage on those it struck.

Now Alvar Fañez Minaya had set the host in order and while the Bishop Don Hieronymo and Gil Diaz led away the body of the Cid, and Doña Ximena, and the baggage, he fell upon the Moors. First he attacked the tents of that Moorish Queen the Negress, who lay nearest to the city; and this onset was so sudden, that they killed full a hundred and fifty Moors before they had time to take arms or go to horse. But that Moorish Negress was so skilful in drawing the Turkish bow, that it was held for a marvel, and it is said that they called her in Arabic *Nugueymat Turya*, which is to say, the Star of the Archers. And she was the first that got on horseback, and with some fifty that were with her, did some hurt to the company of the Cid; but in fine they slew her, and her people fled to the camp. And so great was the uproar and confusion, that few there were who took arms, but instead thereof they turned their backs and fled toward the sea. And when King Bucar and his Kings saw this they were astonished. And it seemed to them that there came against them on the part of the Christians full seventy thousand knights, all as white as snow: and before them a knight of great stature upon a white horse with a bloody cross, who bore in one hand a white banner, and in the other a sword which seemed to be of fire, and he made a great mortality among the Moors who were flying. And King Bucar and the other Kings were so greatly dismayed that they never checked the reins till they had ridden into the sea; and the company of the Cid rode after them, smiting and slaying and giving them no respite; and they smote down so many that it was marvellous, for the Moors did not turn their heads to defend themselves. And when they came to the sea, so great was the press among them to get to the ships, that more than ten thousand died in the water. And of the six and thirty Kings, twenty and two were slain. And King Bucar and they who escaped with him hoisted sails and went their way, and never more turned their heads.

Bibliography

Many versions exist of the *Poema del Cid*. Those translations used in the preparation of this volume are as follows:

Hamilton, R. & Perry, J. *The Poem of the Cid* Penguin, London, 1984.

Merwin, W.S. *The Poem of the Cid* Dent, London, 1959.

Simpson, L.B. *The Poem of the Cid* University of California Press, 1957.

Southey, R. *Chronicle of the Cid* Routledge, London, 1883.

Other commentaries referred to included:

Arnoux, A. *La Legend du Cid Campeador* Club des Libraries de France, 1960.

Hook, D. 'The Conquest of Valencia' in *Cantar de mio Cid* pp120–26. Bulletin of Hispanic Studies, Vol. 50, 1973.

Merwin, W.S. *Some Spanish Ballads* Abelard Schumann, 1961.

Pidal, R.M. *The Cid & His Spain* (trans. Sunderland, H.), John Murray, London, 1934.

Spence, L. *Legends and Romances of Spain* Harrap, London, 1920.

Vilar, P. *Spain, A Brief History* Pergamon Press, Oxford, 1967.

GENEALOGY OF CHARACTERS

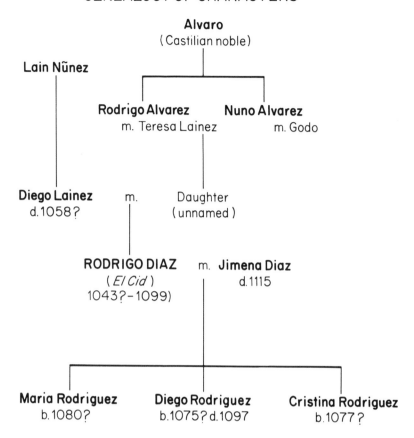

Alvaro
(Castilian noble)

Lain Nūnez

Rodrigo Alvarez
m. Teresa Lainez

Nuno Alvarez
m. Godo

Diego Lainez
d.1058?

m.

Daughter
(unnamed)

RODRIGO DIAZ
(*El Cid*)
1043?-1099)

m. Jimena Diaz
d.1115

Maria Rodriguez
b.1080?

Diego Rodriguez
b.1075? d.1097

Cristina Rodriguez
b.1077?

THE KINGS OF CASTILLE AND LEON

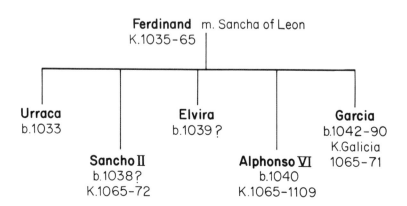

Ferdinand
K.1035-65

m. Sancha of Leon

Urraca
b.1033

Elvira
b.1039?

Garcia
b.1042-90
K.Galicia
1065-71

Sancho II
b.1038?
K.1065-72

Alphonso VI
b.1040
K.1065-1109

Barbarossa

SCOURGE OF EUROPE

BARBAROSSA'S GERMANY 1190

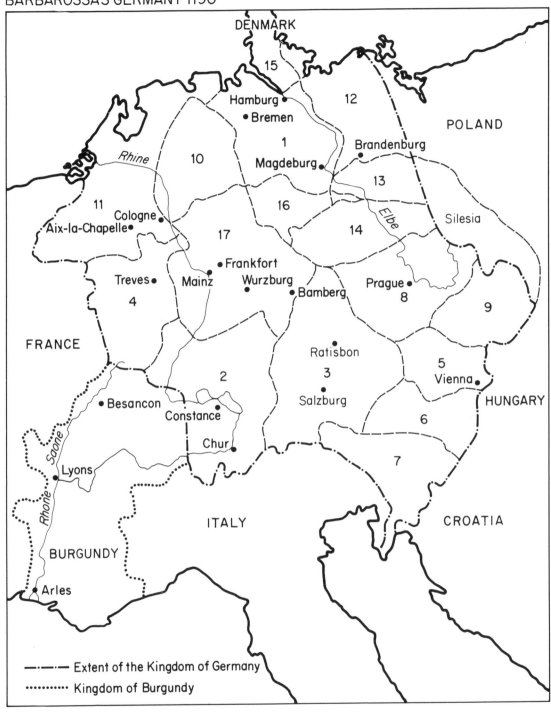

DENMARK

15

Hamburg •

• Bremen

12

POLAND

Rhine

10

1

Magdeburg •

Brandenburg •

13

11

Cologne •

16

Elbe

Silesia

Aix-la-Chapelle •

17

14

Treves •

Mainz •

• Frankfort

Wurzburg •

Prague •

4

• Bamberg

8

9

FRANCE

Besancon •

2

Ratisbon •

3

5

Vienna •

Constance •

Salzburg •

6

HUNGARY

Chur •

7

Lyons •

ITALY

CROATIA

BURGUNDY

Arles •

—·—·— Extent of the Kingdom of Germany

·········· Kingdom of Burgundy

----- Boundary of the various Duchies within Germany

1	Saxony	7	Carinthia	12	March of Brandenburg
2	Swabia	8	Bohemia	13	March of Lusatia
3	Bavaria	9	Moravia	14	March of Misnia
4	Upper Lorraine	10	Westphalia	15	County of Holstein
5	Austria	11	Lower Lorraine and Duchy of Brabant	16	Landgraviate of Thuringia
6	Styria			17	Franconia (several counties)

Emperor and Legend

The Emperor Frederick I drew his popular names of Barbarossa or Rothbart from his red coloured beard. Born in 1121, son of Frederick, Duke of the German territory of Swabia, he became one of the most powerful and famous of the medieval emperors. In addition to his political and military achievements, Barbarossa acquired a legendary fame; like the British King Arthur, he is said to be sleeping, awaiting the time of greatest need for his return as a national saviour.

Throughout his life, Barbarossa strove vigorously to restore and strengthen the Holy Roman Empire. Much of his energy was spent in repeated feuds with various popes, with the Italian confederacy known as the Lombard League, and with his cousin the other great German prince of the period, Henry the Lion. Despite Barbarossa's will and energy, his plans fell apart immediately upon his sudden death; the tragedy of such an able ruler drowning while on crusade shook the entire system which he strove to uphold.

Barbarossa was, in many ways, the epitome of the feudal emperor or prince: he was physically fit and imposing in appearance, he was skilled in arms and he was a great leader and tactician. He fought many successful campaigns, both in terms of warfare and diplomacy, and most of all he upheld the medieval system of fervent religious belief combined with regal authority. He was also a builder and developer of culture, and worked endlessly to set Germany upon a firm governmental and financial footing after the internal struggles that had long divided the German territories against one another.

This was a period of rapid development in the technology and tactics of warfare; gone were the Frankish troops of the time of Charlemagne, who were expected to be riders, foot soldiers, swordsmen, spearsmen and archers all at once. Specialisation, both within class distinctions and within armed skills, was clearly evident and the rigid feudal pattern of government and loyalty and the honour code of vassalage and service which held the culture together, provided various levels of authority in any army, with ultimate leadership from the king or emperor. Mailed and heavily armed knights were an upper military class, with associated

Knight, mounting his horse, wearing chain mail of the type developed from eastern sources during Barbarossa's reign.

99

Body armour, prior to the advent of chain mail, as worn by a helmeted knight in a manuscript illustration of the Barbarossa period.

servants who undertook the many tasks needed to maintain both knight, horse and arms, before and after a conflict.

Foot soldiers bore the brunt of the fighting, not as the light, multi-purpose troops that the original Frankish warriors had tended to be, but divided into functional roles such as lightly armoured spearsmen or archers. There were also sergeants or armigers who were mounted warriors, upon light horses, with light armour, and of a lower social status than the other mounted fighting men. Above these were the heavily armed cavalry, who were free vassals of noble blood. These were the knights of medieval chivalry so well known through courtly fiction, but based upon historical fact.

In a short study it is impossible to deal in depth with the vastly complex web of politics that surrounded Barbarossa; a glance at the list of popes shows just how complex the situation was; hardly had any pope become established and negotiations opened, than another was taking his place. The religious political factor was merely one of several major recurring problems during Barbarossa's reign, all of which interacted with one another. His entire life was involved with warfare, plots and counter-plots, intrigues, feuds and religious problems. We are fortunate to have a letter from Barbarossa himself, written to his biographer, in which he tells of his campaigns in Italy and of the terrible slaughter that resulted from feuds between the Emperor and the Italian cities.

After his death, Barbarossa became the subject of many legends, including that of the sleeping king waiting to return and save his people. Some examples of these stories are included, collected from German oral tradition in the nineteenth century.

Frederick of the Red Beard

Frederick was a Hohenstaufen, and the second emperor to be crowned from this noble family. The Hohenstaufen were descendants of Frederick of Beuren (died 1094), whose son, another Frederick, built the considerable power and fortune of the family before his death in 1105. The Hohenstaufen castle was near Beuren, in the Goeppingen district, east of Stuttgart.

Frederick of Hohenstaufen had two sons: the younger one became Emperor Conrad III, while his first, Frederick the One-Eyed, was the father of Barbarossa. Because of the repeated use of the name Frederick, it is easiest to identify Frederick Barbarossa by his nickname. The Hohenstaufen family were allied to the Babenburgs, originally from Bamberg in Bavaria. Leopold of Babenburg, who was ruler of the Austrian March, married Agnes, the widow of Frederick of Hohen-

Barbarossa with his sons Henry and Frederick in the 1188 manuscript from Fulda Abbey.

staufen, and they had three sons: Leopold, Henry Jasomirgott and Otto von Freising.

Thus Barbarossa came from a noble family, with a background that suited him to his eventual imperial career. In 1147 he succeeded to the dukedom of Swabia, and within a year he set out to take part in the Second Crusade, under the command of his uncle Conrad III and Louis VII of France.

One of the most illuminating insights into the character of Frederick Barbarossa comes from the descriptions of him in the Fourth Book of Bishop Otto von Freising and from Rahewin, his twelfth-century biographer.

The descriptions are a mixture of quotations from texts which were already known at the time of writing, when Rahewin completed the work of Otto von Freising. These are mixed freely with original descriptive material. The descriptions therefore are also found in earlier works dealing with Theodoric II of the Visigoths, Charlemagne, and other historical characters. The copying of descriptions of famous men from other chronicles is typical of the style of the period, and need not be taken to imply lack of information or plagiarism, for wherever necessary personal details are added. The process is similar to oral tradition, in which good descriptions, tales, or verses are preserved and repeated; indeed the audience or reader would have been disappointed if some of the famous and much loved descriptions were not included.

Apart from the deliberate references to Theodoric and Charlemagne, which are intended to show that Frederick Barbarossa was of the same mould as these great heroes, the description of the Kaiserslauten palace is especially interesting. When examining Barbarossa as a legendary char-

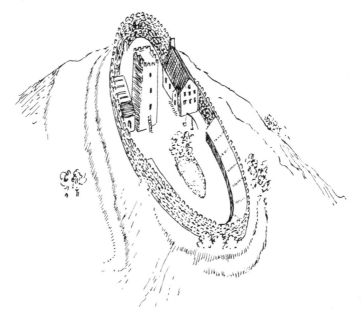

Reconstruction from archaelogical evidence of the original Staufen Castle.

102

acter, this image appears again, from a traditional source collected by the Grimm brothers in the nineteenth century. Apart from the obvious literary currency of descriptions of this sort, it is significant that a garden, palace, or type of paradise is always associated with the sleeping king or emperor, for this is the ancient motif found in classical mythology of the Titan Cronos, ruling in the Golden Age.

Whatever else, the mixture is a fascinating glimpse of the great German ruler:

'Divine august Frederick is in character and appearance such man that he deserves to be studied even by those not in close contact with him. Both God and nature have combined to bestow lavishly upon him the gift of perfect happiness. His character is one that not even those envious of his power can disparage him. His body is well proportioned. He is shorter than the tallest of men, yet taller and more noble than those of middle height. His hair is golden and curls a little above his forehead. His ears are only just covered by his hair above, as the barber, out of respect for the empire, keeps the hair in his head and cheeks short by continual trimming.

'His eyes are sharp and piercing, his nose well formed, his beard reddish, his lips fine and not pulled out of shape by too long a mouth. His entire visage is bright and cheerful. His teeth are even a snow white in colour. The skin of his throat and neck, which is stout but not fat, is milky white and often imbued with the red glow of youth; modesty not anger causes him to blush frequently. His shoulders are broad and he is strongly built. His thighs supported by stocky calves are neat and sturdy.

'His pace is firm and steady, his voice clear, and his entire bearing manly. Because of his shape he has an air of dignity and power, standing or sitting. His health is very good, except that he is sometimes subject to an occasional fever. He is a lover of warfare, but only in the pursuit of peace. He is quick of hand, extremely wise in counsel, merciful to suppliants, and kind to those taken in under his protection.

'You may ask about his daily routine when abroad; he attends matins at church and priestly services either alone or with a small following, and worships so devoutly that he has set an example to all Italians of the honour and reverence that should be paid to bishops and clergy. He shows such a deep respect for divine services that he honours with seemly silence every hour in which psalms are sung to God, nor does anyone dare meanwhile to trouble him with matters of state. When his devotions are over, after the Mass, having been blessed by holy relics, he then dedicates the rest of the morning to the work of government of his empire.

'If he engages in hunting he is foremost in training, assessing, and using horses, dogs, falcons and other hunting birds. He strings his own bow while hunting, takes the arrows, sets and fires them. If you choose what to hit, he will hit whatever you have chosen.

'At meals there is both restraint and royal bounty; moderate drinking prevails without excess, yet those who hunger will never complain of frugality. When it is time for recreation, he sets aside his regal dignity for a moment, and is in such a humour that his condescension cannot be criticised, his severity cannot be called bloodthirsty.

'Towards his household he is not threatening nor is he contemptuous of counsel when offered, nor vindictive when searching out a fault. He earnestly reads the Scriptures and adventures of ancient kings. He usually distributes with his own hands alms to the poor, and carefully divides a tithe of his wealth among the churches and monasteries. He is very eloquent in his mother tongue, but understands Latin more readily than he actually speaks it. He wears his native costume, is neither extravagant or frivolous in his clothing, nor is he ever poorly dressed. It pleases him to have his camp display the signs of Mars rather than those of Venus.

'Though he is famous for the extension of his territories and conquests in which he is constantly engaged, he has also started many public works for the beauty and convenience of the realm; some of these he has completed, and a great part of his wealth is set aside for pious honouring of his ancestors. For he has fittingly restored the most beautiful places built long ago by Charles the Great at Nijmegen and near the village of Ingelheim, adorned with acclaimed workmanship – structures extremely well built but decaying through neglect and age. By this he gives clear evidence of his innate greatness of soul. At Kaiserslauten he built a royal palace of red stone on a lavish scale. On one side it was surrounded by a strong wall, on the other it was washed by a fish pond the size of lake, well stocked with all kinds of fish and game birds, to feast both the eye and the palate. It has close to it a park that provides pasture for a large

herd of deer and wild goats. The regal splendour of all these works and
their abundance, too great to list further, are well worth seeing.'

Twelfth Century Germany

Frederick Barbarossa's exploits are all the more interesting in the context
of the type of society into which he was born. This society moulded
many of the ideals, virtues, strengths and weaknesses in his later role as
emperor.

German Medieval Culture

Twelfth-century Germany was in a period of expansion; the population
was increasing rapidly, agriculture and trade were booming, and towns
were growing substantially. During this period, the city of Cologne
became the biggest city in Germany, with a population of around 50,000
people by 1180, and extensive trade connections. It also became the

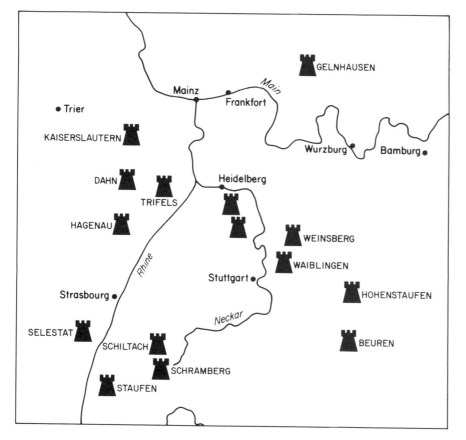

Barbarossa initiated a programme of castle construction in order
to strengthen imperial power in
Germany.

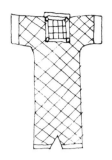

Barbarossa's common soldiers were almost certainly still wearing Norman-style hauberks as late as the Third Crusade.

largest city in Western Europe, with walls enclosing an area of no fewer than 483 acres.

During his youth, Barbarossa saw a rapid increase in the number of monasteries, considerable development of learning, scientific and intellectual skills, and the beginning of cathedral schools, which were soon to blossom into universities. By the end of the twelfth century, there were universities across Europe; at Oxford. Montpelier, Paris, Salerno and Bologna. There were also rapid developments in military techniques, which Barbaross had ample opportunity to employ during his many campaigns.

An important outlet for the growing population, energy and skills of the period were the crusades – religious wars against the Saracens, aiming to free Christian shrines, particularly Jerusalem, from Muslim rule.

Feudal Loyalty

Loyalty to specific lords was an essential aspect of medieval life, running from the most humble serf, who was virtually a possession or slave, to the bond between vassal and lord that held the entire culture together at the highest levels. This is well illustrated by a famous decree made by Barbarossa, in which he ruled that a fire raiser who had taken refuge in a castle must be delivered to justice by those who had sheltered him, but not if he were the lord of the castle-owner, or his vassal, or his kinsman. The feudal bond of duty and loyalty was seen to be almost as strong as, and certainly similar to, the ties of blood relationship.

In contrast to this complex and long-established system, which originally derived from the tribal period in early Celtic and Germanic Europe, we find that certain cities and merchants were freed of feudal ties. Liberties were conferred on cities, in order that feudal laws should not restrict trade and other important aspects of mercantile power. Many cities had rights of self-government, with councils replacing feudal governors. Much of Barbarossa's continual political conflict was connected to administrative matters of this sort.

Feudal service had strict rules, terms and periods, with specific requirements for nobles and serving man alike. The system also perpetuated the concept of the code of honour, in which the strong defended the weak against oppressors, and the highest rulers were always benevolent towards their vassals.

More typical though is this armour from an illustration of around 1190. One warrior wears a helmet with a nasal guard and carries a spear with cross pieces.

The Second Crusade

The Second Crusade was organised by Pope Eugenius III, but was not a success. The planning and organisation were inefficient, and although it was supposedly undertaken as a Christian venture, the Byzantine Emperor Manuel Commenus obstructed the crusade whenever possible.

Newly appointed as Duke of Swabia, Frederick Barbarossa had an opportunity to mix with other nobles, and acquitted himself well in the crusade. His loyalty and courage earned him the friendship and confidence of Emperor Conrad III. He was also able to meet and fight along with his relatives, Otto von Freising, Henry Jasomirgott, Henry, Bishop of Ratisbon, and Vladislav, Duke of Bohemia.

This unfortunate crusade was not a total loss as far as Barbarossa was concerned, for it set the political and feudal scene for his election as Emperor within a short time of his return to Germany. The system of government to which he was elected had an interesting structure and development.

Government of Twelfth-century Germany
The central chain of command and influence was as follows:
The Emperor
Kings and princes
Lesser noble vassals and feudal lords
Special governors and appointees (often placed directly by the Emperor)

Medieval representation of Frederick Barbarossa as a crusader, the role in which he met his death.

THE ADMINISTRATION
Chancellor in Chief of Germany (usually Archbishop of Mainz)
Chancellor in Chief of Italy (usually Archbishop of Cologne)
Chancellor in Chief of Burgundy (usually Archbishop of Besançon)
Administration at county level was undertaken by the feudal lords.

THE COURT
Counsellors
Relatives
Friends and favourites
Court Officials were the Seneschal, Cup-bearer, Marshal and Chamberlain. These were ancient, traditional positions and could be of considerable power depending upon the individuals and the emperor himself.

The Diet represented both central and local authorities, and was a gathering of major importance.

Armour and Weapons

The reign of Frederick Barbarossa saw some important developments in military equipment, particularly in the design of armour. To grasp the overall picture of the weaponry and armour available to the knights and soldiers of Barbarossa's armies, one must summarise the development of equipment during the period concerned, bearing in mind that any changes were not universal and immediate, and that arms and armour of both older and more recent styles would have happily co-existed.

Hand Weapons

Fourteen types of shafted weapons carried by Barbarossa's campaigning armies; military flails (1, 6, 7), marteau (2); battle axe (3), fauchards (4, 8), corcesque (5), military fork (9), halberd (10), partisan (11) and guisarmes (12, 13).

The basic weapons in use from the end of the eleventh century to the end of the twelfth century were the spear or lance, the mace, the bow, the sword and dagger. Variant weapons included the guisarme or fauchard, which persisted in many forms as late as the seventeenth century, and inflicted such horrible wounds that attempts were made to have it banned during the medieval period. The pole-axe was a long-shafted fighting axe requiring the use of both hands, while the standard battle-axe could be wielded single handed. The axe was originally a northern European weapon, and a typical design during the time of Barbarossa would have been a simple axe blade balanced by a spike on its reverse.

Northern European warriors also used the halberd, which consisted of an axe blade balanced by a pick, with the head of the shaft terminating in a long, vicious spike. The halberd was not introduced extensively into England or France until as late as the fourteenth century, but may well have been used by the Germanic troops of Barbarossa, particularly those vassals from the more northerly territories.

Towards the close of the twelfth century the pike was used to counter cavalry charges, and remained in use in various forms until as late as the eighteenth century. It consisted of a long, narrow, steel spear head, with a long wooden shaft reinforced by strips of metal. The butt end of the pike was fitted with an iron shoe which could be grounded to take the shock of a charge, and the metal strips along the shaft (sometimes as much as 20 feet long though usually around 10 feet) acted as protection against sword cuts.

The fork was simply a military development of the agricultural implement. It usually had two or three prongs of deliberately unequal length with hooks added to pull horsemen down, and sometimes barbs. As with a number of shafted weapons, it was used from the eleventh to the seventeenth century. Scaling forks were made with long shafts and prominent hooks to dislodge defenders from walls. The bill was a shafted weapon with a crescent-shaped blade sharpened on the inside; it was current from the ninth century onwards in various forms and, like the fork, had an agricultural origin as an improvised weapon which gradually became specialised in its own right. It was popularly known as the 'brown bill' because such improvised weapons were often rusty. The glaive was another variant of the bill, but its cutting edge was along the convex curve of the blade rather than the concave; this weapon also developed hooks and spurs on the base of the blade for specialist purposes. The glaive was very popular in both France and Germany, and the word 'glaive' was frequently used to mean any knife or blade attached to a shaft.

The morning star or *morgenstern* was a German weapon, used by both cavalry and infantry. The infantry version had a longer shaft, but both versions were essentially spiked maces. The Germanic cavalry often had morning stars made entirely of iron.

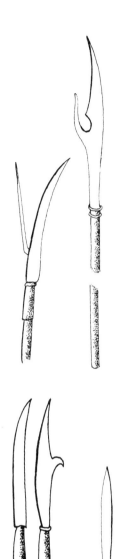

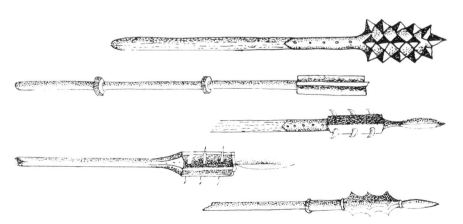

Guisarmes (top) were used to great effect as thrusting and cutting weapons on long shafts whilst (above) the cultellus was used to administer the coup de grace to unhorsed knights, and the war scythe and glaive to pull the horsemen from his saddle. Other hand-held weapons of the time (left) were the morning star or morgenstern, mace and goedendag.

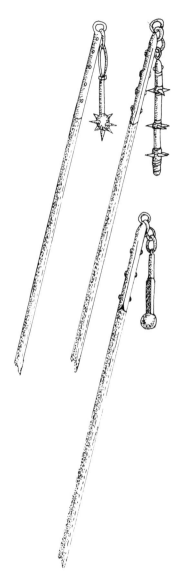

Other ferocious hand weapons were the 'holy water sprinklers' or military flails.

A close relative of the *morgenstern* was the aptly named 'holy water sprinkler', more prosaically known as the military flail. This consisted of a long or short shaft with a staple at the end, to which a chain was attached. The chain terminated in an iron ball covered with spikes; a variant form had the chain supporting a wooden or iron flail sprouting spikes.

The mace, or goedendag, was a weapon used throughout Europe up to the sixteenth century. Many variant forms existed, but the basic shape was a central weighted head surrounded by flanges, sometimes with a spike for thrusting. In later centuries the mace was to become an emblem of authority, and is still used by town councils and corporations in Europe as a ceremonial implement. The mace was particularly favoured by militant churchmen, who argued that although the scriptures forbade the shedding of blood, and thus precluded them from wielding swords, the mace was a crushing implement and thus avoided such religious bans altogether.

The *martel de fer* was a type of mace used by both horse and foot soldiers, and was often carried by archers in preference to the sword. It consisted of a shaft with a hammer head, often serrated, and balanced by a pick or blade on the opposite side.

The sword hardly varied in form from the twelfth to the fifteenth century: it generally had a two-edged blade, about 40 inches in length. The quillons were usually straight, but occasionally curved towards the blade; the grip was sometimes double handed and sometimes single; pommels tended to be decorated, particularly those of noblemen and princes.

Other weapons found between approximately 1066 and 1180 include the bisacuta, oucin and besaque, all of which were types of pick used to pierce the joints between the armour plates on a hauberk. Foot soldiers used daggers extensively to disable unhorsed knights; these daggers were known as *cultelli* and occasionally approached the length of a short sword. Guisarmes, mentioned earlier, were also fitted with bells to frighten horses, a fact which emphasises the general style of warfare in which the foot and mounted warriors continually strove to outdo one another. Debate as to the relative merits of foot and horse continued for many centuries, and still exists in an attenuated form in the modern technological army.

Arbalests and Crossbows

Although the crossbow is known to have existed as early as the fourth century, its main use was as a hunting weapon and it was not until the latter part of the twelfth century that it became a major military weapon. However, this was not without some opposition: in 1139 a council presided over by Pope Innocent II banned the crossbow as a barbarous weapon unfit for Christian use, a decision confirmed by Innocent III.

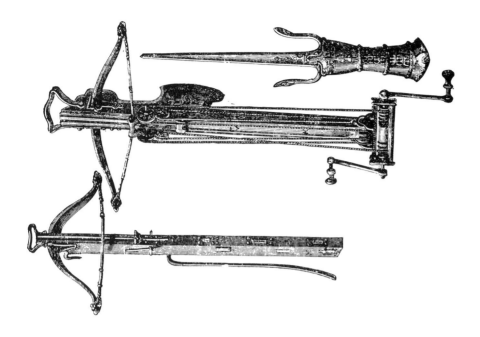

Richard I of England allowed the use of crossbows during the crusade, but in England the famous longbow eventually took precedence. On the Continent the arbalest or crossbow was used extensively, and crossbowmen often formed an individual armoured unit, both for defensive purposes and as a serious threat to charging cavalry.

Hand crossbow, rolling purchase arbalest and Moorish three-pointed dagger; all used on the crusades and during Barbarossa's Italian campaigns.

Early Armour, Shields and Helmets

Body armour varied enormously; earlier forms in the eleventh century tended to be scale armour, in which reinforcement was added to a leather garment. The reinforcements could be bronze, leather, iron, horn, or *cuir-bouilli* which was an extremely hard, boiled and moulded leather. Quilting was another form of body armour, in which the overgarment was padded with wool or cloth sewn between two layers of fabric. This provided a good defence against swords and arrows, but no protection against a lance thrust or a mace. Quilting was also used underneath mail and metal armour, as an additional defence layer and as padding for comfort against chafing. Common foot soldiers, however, often had quilting as their only armour.

Shields lengthened during the period concerned, and the Norman-style long shield, bowed to give extra area and defensive shape, was a standard design. Germanic foot soldiers still used small circular shields, similar to those of their Frankish predecessors.

Helmets were frequently of the standard conical shape, fitted with a nasal strip. The nasal strip was popular until the middle of the twelfth century, when it dropped out of general use. Neck and cheek guards

The crossbowman, or arbalastier, shown here wears helmet and sword of the Moorish influence which appeared in the early 1200s.

III

The German pot helmet developed rapidly from this basic form.

were also known on helmets, though these were less widespread. The heaume or pot helmet appeared late in the twelfth century, eventually developing into a complete head covering. This type became increasingly common and more ornate in the two following centuries.

The Chain Mail Revolution

By the latter half of the twelfth century, when the crusades were in full swing, chain mail replaced the simpler scale armour to a great extent, and the pot helmet was increasingly used by the wealthier warriors. Chain mail was an eastern technology, and the crude Western version made from bands or rings fared badly when compared to the light, skilfully-made mail of the oriental cavalry during the crusading period. The Saracen warriors were able to ride and fight with far more comfort and freedom than their European adversaries. The best chain mail in the Christian armies was, at first, that looted from the Saracens. A general improvement of European mail occurred due to this influence, but true chain mail was expensive, and the almost exclusive property of the lords and princes.

Germany and Spain were eventually to become major producers of armour: within a century or so of the time of Barbarossa some of the most famous makers of armour were German, while Cologne became renowned for its swords. This last speciality may reflect the much earlier skills of the Franks, the Frankish swords were of such good quality that the Emperor Charlemagne issued an edict that they were not to be exported. Thirteenth- and fourteenth-century German arms and armour, however, were extensively sold all over Europe.

The foot soldiers, however, did not benefit from looted oriental mail, or from the Western revolution in home manufacture. They still used the simpler armour found from the preceding century, with conical helmets padded or plated hauberks or jerkins, and fought with unprotected legs.

Barbarossa's foot soldiers were often still attired like this eleventh-century warrior.

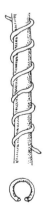

Chain mail was made first by coiling links around a pole and then fully constructed by interlinking.

Barbarossa's troops subdue the Roman mob at the time of his coronation. The violent citizens sought to kill or abduct the Pope when Barbarossa refused to pay them an immense bribe.

Foot soldiers storming a platform defended by a crossbowman in heavy armour. The attackers carry a siege hook, bow, sling, and axe and all combatants utilise armour and weaponry of the period.

Engines of War

The taking and destroying of fortified towns played a considerable part in the many campaigns and siege warfare of the medieval period. Projectile weapons had been known from Roman times, but much of the technology was redeveloped during the crusades. It may be surprising to discover that medieval war engines were capable of throwing huge objects, and causing extensive destruction within a besieged city. Roman weapons used the bow as their mechanical basis, but the medieval ones tended to use the sling, which made them heavier and more cumbersome.

Slinging siege engines used in the twelfth century had long wooden arms powered by heavy weights. These then developed into the trebuchet, which had a sling at one end of a long wooden arm. Trebuchets had a long range, and were generally constructed on site. In addition to stones, they fired pitch, naphtha, Greek fire, dead horses and other animals, and barrels of putrid, rotting matter. The putrid matter was intended to cause plague in the besieged town or castle.

The trebuchet; a twelfth-century example of this deadly weapon, capable of enormous destruction as a siege engine.

Although the English savant Roger Bacon deciphered the composition of gunpowder in the thirteenth century, it was used in the twelfth by the Moors in wars in Spain and so was probably known to the troops of Barbarossa, perhaps as a terrible Moorish secret weapon.

In conclusion, it is clear that from this examination of the state of weaponry and warfare throughout the reign of Barbarossa, and given that he lived to the age of 70, he must have experienced many of the gradual changes and improvements in arms and armour that occurred during the twelfth century. Of particular relevance to Barbarossa as Emperor was the use of the chain mail stolen from the Saracens, and the resulting changes in European manufacture that followed.

Barbarossa was crowned Emperor in Saint Peter's Basilica, declaring that the Pope merely confirmed his existing right to imperial power, but opposed by the Roman citizens and surrounding Italian territories.

The Emperor's First Plan

In 1152 Emperor Conrad III died at Bamberg. At this time heirs were not selected exclusively through primogeniture, but by election. In any case, Conrad's son Henry, who the nobles had agreed to elect upon his father's death, had himself died. So when Conrad III handed the royal insignia to his nephew Barbarossa upon his death bed, no clearer signal was required of a potential choice, and the German princes, anxious to elect a suitable person of their own choice before any papal interference could be made, chose Frederick Barbarossa. The conflict between nobility, emperor and papacy was to be a constant and powerful factor throughout his reign. Within a few days of his election, Barbarossa was crowned on the 9th March 1152. The ceremony took place in Aachen (Aix-la-Chapelle), the imperial city developed extensively by Charlemagne.

At the time of his election, Barbarossa was aged 28; he was athletic, and excelled in swimming, riding and hunting. He was of medium height, with broad shoulders, and, of course, his famous fair complexion and red beard. Proven as a warrior, he also exemplified many of the feudal virtues so important to his culture and class: loyalty, justice and, where necessary, inflexibility.

It should be clearly stated that Barbarossa was pious; his entire life and style of rule was guided by his religious beliefs. He practised Christian morals, and took a very active role in the development and protection of the Church. However, his complex arguments and bitter feuds with the Holy See were in the realm of politics; kings, emperors and popes were well practised in setting aside or utilising matters of faith and devotion when it came to controlling the apparatus of temporal power.

Most important of all was Barbarossa's inherent intelligence; he was no mere warrior king or religious enthusiast. He understood and developed the concepts of imperial rule and responsibility, and took an intense interest in all matters of law, government and the practical realisation of the feudal ideals which he personally embodied. It was that very intelligence which evolved the master strategies.

Warrior in tegulated, square-plate armour of the late eleventh century.

Shipboard warriors of Barbarossa's army carrying staff slings and fire arrows; a battle axe, spear and sword are also in evidence.

The Revealed Plan

Barbarossa's initial aim was to unify Germany, and settle a number of conflicts which had been weakening the realm. This was to be the first of three stages in a carefully planned development of the imperial role and power.

In 1152, the first plan was revealed by the new emperor. He wrote to various important and powerful persons, including, of course, the pope, Eugenius III, declaring that he would, upon his honour, re-establish the strength and purpose of Germany and the empire. In short, he sought to restore the Holy Roman Empire of Germany, Burgundy and Italy.

In 1153 an agreement of mutual assistance was signed, in which Eugenius III and Barbarossa confirmed support for one another, or more significantly between pope and emperor. Unfortunately, Eugenius died on the 8th July of the same year, and was succeeded by Anastasius IV. The new pope was still pro-imperial, but did not survive for long, dying on the 3rd December 1154. The variations in papal power and support are so crucial to an understanding of Barbarossa's reign that the summary of papal allegiances included is worthy of study and is useful in following the complex developments.

First Italian Campaign

Barbarossa's declared and overall intention was to purify, restore and develop the Holy Roman Empire. Germany was within his immediate control, and Burgundy was the least of the three kingdoms which he resolved to merge firmly together, but Italy was a hotbed of revolt, dissent and major political and economic opposition to his aims. Thus, in October of 1154, Barbarossa mounted his first expedition, with the aim of restoring papal authority where it had been challenged, and fully realising the imperial crown.

He was eventually to undertake six campaigns in Lombardy to subdue and punish rebellious cities, grown rich through the boom in manufacturing and commerce, and increasingly independent of the old feudal authority. The immediate cause of his first campaign was to support the town of Lodi, which had been subject to control by Milan. Barbarossa sent a mandate requiring Milan to give up her claims, but the Milanese consuls tore up the document, and the imperial ambassador fled an enraged crowd.

So in 1154 Barbarossa crossed the Alps with a large army and Milan was severely punished. The city of Tortona, which refused to submit, was burnt to the ground and gradual submission was forced upon all the rebellious cities of northern Italy. In 1155 Barbarossa was crowned with the famous Iron Crown of Lombardy, said to have been made from a nail of the True Cross.

By this time the pro-imperial Pope Anastasius had died, and had been succeeded by the anti-imperial Hadrian. The new pope did not share the

Man-at-arms in the type of armour combining leather and iron developed towards the close of Barbarossa's long life.

general goodwill towards Frederick, and wanted to assert the superiority of pope over emperor. While he was not openly aggressive to the strong Barbarossa, he certainly made it clear that he did not wish the emperor to interfere in ecclesiastical matters. Barbarossa, as we have seen, believed it to be his holy duty to weld crown and church together.

A working compromise was reached only after Barbarossa agreed to hold the Pope's bridle and stirrup at a formal meeting; an act of ritual homage which he had at first refused. Meanwhile, the unruly people of Rome, currently opposed to the Pope, suggested that it would suit them better to confirm the imperial crown upon Barbarossa. He replied that he held his power in Italy by the same right of conquest established by Charlemagne and Otto, he had come, he said, 'not to receive as a suppliant the transient favours of an unruly people, but as a prince resolved to claim, if necessary by force of arms, the inheritance of his forebears'.

Thus, on the 18th June 1155, Frederick Barbarossa was finally handed the sword, sceptre and golden crown that declared him fully Emperor, confirmed by military, political and spiritual authority. His first act was to seize possession of the Leonine City in Rome, which came under attack from rebellious Roman citizens based upon the Capitol. But the Emperor and Pope withdrew to Tivoli, where Barbarossa again confirmed papal authority by refusing to accept the keys in his own name. Clearly, he realised that he must uphold the papacy even in the light of Hadrian's opposition to imperial equality.

On 27th July 1155 Barbarossa razed Spoleto, which had paid him tribute earlier in false money. He also put Milan under imperial ban during this period, depriving the powerful city of its regalia and right to mint money or collect tolls. He was gradually moving out of Italy, leaving the Pope to handle his own political problems after an imperial show of strength. But Milan would have to be dealt with again, and Barbarossa would return to quell the troublesome Italians on more than one occasion.

In September of 1155 he finally departed for Germany, to embark upon a further programme of reorganisation in his homeland.

Second Plan – The Great Design

The most important stage of Barbarossa's rule now began to unfold; in this phase he aimed to expand imperial power and to unify Italy, Alsace and Burgundy. His first moves were to settle various internal disputes among his relatives and nobility, ensuring that they were kept satisfied and willing to fulfil their feudal duty to him as supreme overlord.

In May of 1156, Barbarossa appointed a new chancellor. His choice for this important post was unusual, for the chancellor was not a career diplomat or a member of favoured royal chapel, he was, in the courtly sense of the day, an outsider. His name was Rainald von Dassel, and his appointment was to prove crucial to Barbarossa's success. The imperial system of government was well established by the time Barbarossa came to the throne, with the established chain of command already described.

Rainald was a man of considerable talent; he was described by his friends as being generous, serene and sincere. More important from the governmental viewpoint was that he was extremely active and intelligent, a good speaker and a skilled, astute negotiator. Most important of all was the fact that he was devoted to imperial service; thus his role as chancellor and Barbarossa's role as emperor were seldom to come into conflict.

Barbarossa was ever the pragmatist; despite his ambitions, he paid homage to Pope Alexander III.

Although Rainald was a cleric, he did not take his religious vocation with any great seriousness, and on many occasions used his intelligence to give imperial policies an anti-papal effect. He was attracted, though, by ceremony and magical or miraculous powers associated with religion, and when he had the relics of the Three Wise Men brought from Milan to Germany, it was he who carried them into Cologne Cathedral.

Rainald was convinced of divine approval for his role within the imperial cause; his reputation as a soldier was considerable, and he put his skill and courage (which he did not modestly hide) down to the essential 'rightness' of his task. Thus he and Barbarossa were to become close friends as well as working together, for the next ten years. He died in 1167 of plague after the defeat of the army near Tusculum.

Marriage and the Treaty of Benevento

On the 5th June 1156, Frederick Barbarossa married for the second time. His new wife was Beatrice of Burgundy, and the marriage was part of the complex Second Plan to strengthen imperial power. In the twelfth century marriages were generally arranged by parents, guardians or overlords, so this move was quite normal for the time, marriages being primarily matters of finance or territory, rather than of the heart.

Through his marriage to Beatrice, Frederick gained control of Provence and Burgundy entirely, thus strengthening the position of his native Swabia.

Meanwhile, a treaty had been negotiated between Pope Hadrian IV and William I of Sicily (June 1156) in which certain territorial rights were listed, and in return homage and a large yearly tribute were paid to the Pope. This effectively broke the treaty signed between Barbarossa and Pope Eugenius III, and contributed to growing conflict between emperor and papacy.

In August of 1157 Barbarossa invaded Poland to resolve troublesome territorial arguments; and the following month found him holding court at Besançon, one of the imperial centres established by his predecessor Charlemagne. Here the Pope was to further aggravate the already poor relationship between himself and the Emperor. In a complex letter to Frederick, Hadrian implied that the empire was a *beneficium* of the papacy, a gift bestowed only by papal authority. This suggestion was certainly not accepted, and in his reply Frederick Barbarossa made it clear that the empire was independent of the papacy, no matter how closely tied the two entities were through political and religious motives and history.

The reply from Barbarossa, couched in the most vituperative and courtly language, may be summarised by its last section, quoted here from the writings of Otto von Freising, his contemporary chronicler:

Barbarossa's second wife, the Empress Beatrice, depicted on a coin of the period.

And since, through election by the princes, the kingdom and the empire are ours from

God alone, Who at the time of the passion of His Son Christ subjected the world to dominion by the two swords (Luke 22:38) and since the apostle Peter taught this doctrine 'fear God, honour the king' (Peter 2:17) whosoever says that we received the imperial crown as a benefice from the lord pope contradicts the divine ordinance and the doctrine of Peter and is guilty of a lie . . .

Barbarossa's own depiction shows imperial regalia of orb and sceptre.

The Great Design Progresses

By January 1158 Barbarossa was holding a diet at Regensburg to settle internal German disputes. He also sent Rainald von Dassel and Otto von Wittlesbach to Italy as ambassadors. Their task was to take oaths of allegiance from the various semi-independent cities, and to encourage resistance to Milan.

In July of 1158 the Emperor once again led his army into Italy, and by August the troops had reached Milan. With the surrounding countryside devastated, and the common people deprived of all supplies of food, both Brescia and Milan submitted to Frederick's authority, and Milan became an imperial city.

In November of the same year, the important diet of Roncaglia was held, at which all the cities and imperial vassals of Italy were represented. Four of the leading jurists of Bologna were appointed to prepare a document defining for ever the relationship between the empire on one hand and the cities of Italy and imperial vassal on the other. The rights assigned to the empire by these jurists were so great that many cities refused to acknowledge them. Milan prepared for strong resistance to the Roncaglia decrees, which included conceding of all regalia or royal rights to Frederick, such as rents, tolls on roads, rivers, in ports and in market places. The independence of the cities was effectively strangled. As part of the Milanese conspiracy to defy the decrees, a messenger tried unsuccessfully to assassinate Barbarossa in his camp at Lodi in June of 1159.

Death of Hadrian IV

On 1st September 1159, Hadrian IV died. The cardinals, clergy and Roman people were divied into pro- and anti-imperial camps and as a result two competing popes were elected. Frederick supported Victor IV, while his rival, Alexander III, was forced to flee Italy and take refuge in the powerful kingdom of France.

The Razing of Milan

By 1161 Milan was again in revolt, and Barbarossa assembled a large army in Germany, crossed the Alps in the spring, and laid siege to the city. His tactic was to starve the Milanese into submission so the city was encircled by a ring of improvised castles, cutting off communications and supplies. This enabled the Emperor to avoid any pitched battles that would be destructive of manpower, and by 1162 the Milanese were starving and forced into surrender.

It was clear by February that Frederick would allow no compromises; he returned six prisoners to the city, five of whom were blinded, while the sixth had his nose cut off. This last prisoner had been allowed to keep his sight only in order to lead the others home as a terrible example. Milan agreed to accept the Roncaglia decrees, and agreed to the appointment of a *podesta*. Such officials were occasionally native Lombards, but more often were German country squires or minor nobility, proven warriors and trusted servants of Barbarossa. Unfortunately, they often had little experience in civil administration and although the system may have seemed effective in suppressing Lombard leadership, ultimately it acted against Frederick's interests due to its inherent inefficiency and unpopularity. In this case, however, unconditional surrender was now required.

In March of 1162, Milan was razed to the ground by imperial troops, and the inhabitants were forced to settled in four widespread parts of the territory. The city was not rebuilt until 1167. By this dramatic and merciless conquest, Barbarossa pacified northern Italy, placing the territory under an imperial governor.

The Papal Schism

Frederick now attempted to have his approved pope, Victor, recognised by Louis VII of France, and both he and Rainald made speeches at the

synod at St Jean-de-Losne declaring that the Emperor had sole authority to decide a papal election. This did not meet with approval, and by 1163 Frederick had returned to Italy with a small band of men, aiming to capture Rome and proceed to Sicily. Meanwhile Alexander III formed a new league of Italian cities from his refuge in France, and fomented further revolts.

In 1164, Victor died at Lucca, and the dubious consecration of Paschal III, soon known as the 'anti-pope', was carried out by Bishop Henry of Liege. This consecration was arranged by Rainald, for blatantly political reasons, and at first Frederick would not accept such an obvious ploy on the part of his chancellor to gain control of papal authority. But the German church now supported the rival Alexander, as they had not been consulted over the appointment of Paschal.

In 1164, Rainald was deprived of the chancellery, but retained his position as Arch-chancellor for Italy. It was in this role that he removed the relics of the Three Wise Men from Milan, and placed them in Cologne Cathedral, where they are still found to this day.

Henry the Lion

The dominance of the figure of Frederick Barbarossa makes it easy to lose sight of other major characters who lived during his reign. One individual who demands special attention is Henry the Lion, leader of the

Guelphs. The supporters of Barbarossa became known as Ghibellines from the name of the Hohenstaufen castle, Waiblingen; and the opposition were known as Guelphs, from the Welfs, traditional enemies of the house of Hohenstaufen.

Henry was one of the most remarkable princes of Germany in the twelfth century. Born in 1129, he inherited large territories and an equally large collection of feuds when his father was poisoned in 1139. By 1146 Henry had become ruler of Saxony.

At the diet of princes in Frankfurt (1147) he demanded the return of Bavaria, which had been taken from his father by Emperor Conrad III and bestowed upon an Austrian vassal. Conrad refused, and war broke out between the Guelph faction and the emperor.

In 1152, with the death of Conrad, Germany was deeply divided. The houses of Hohenstaufen (Ghibellines) and Welf (Guelphs) both pressed their claims to the royal crown but as already described, Frederick Barbarossa succeeded in his claim. Despite this rivalry the new Emperor restored Bavaria to Henry in 1154, bringing him to the height of his power as a German prince.

The year 1165 also saw growing unrest in Saxony, where Henry as leader of the Guelphs, had gradually increased his power and field of influence, originally with the encouragement of his imperial overlord Frederick. A strong coalition developed against Henry, including Rainald, Albrecht the Bear, the Landgraf Ludwig of Thuringia, and many lesser vassals from Saxony, Thuringia and Hessen. Thus, internal unrest once again threatened Barbarossa's concept of the great design.

In fact, Henry the Lion ruled territories extending from the Baltic and the North Sea to the Adriatic, but his period of favour and amicable relationship with Barbarossa was not to last long. Those first signs of unrest were found in disputes with various powerful churchmen, who formed a confederacy against him at Merseburg in 1166.

Within two years of overcoming this faction, Henry had divorced his first wife and married Matilda, the daughter of Henry II of England. He then travelled on an expedition to the Holy Land, and in his absence his various enemies,including the Emperor himself, began to encroach upon his territories. By 1174 Henry returned to Germany to serve under his imperial overlord on the fifth campaign in Italy.

In this campaign he led a large body of troops, as befitted such a powerful prince, but due to the continuing disputes between himself and Barbarossa, he abandoned the imperial cause at the siege of Allessandria. As a result of this disloyalty, and his refusal to appear at three imperial diets, he was banished from the empire and his dominions were distributed among other princes and powerful vassals loyal to Barbarossa. After a period of conflict, Henry was forced to accept the ban, and fled to his father-in-law in England.

In 1182, he asked formally for pardon, prostrating himself before

The Hohenstaufen castle of Trifels, one of Barbarossa's family strongholds in the Rhineland.

122

Barbarossa. In return he was promised his hereditary possessions of Luneburg and Brunswick, but ordered to leave Germany for three years, and so returned to England. By 1184 he was back in Germany, ruling his hereditary territories in peace, but with a much reduced status.

However, Barbarossa was still suspicious of the leader of the Guelphs, and when he resolved to go on crusade he ordered that Henry must either follow him to the Holy Land or return to exile in England for a further three years. Henry chose England, but because the imperial promise to preserve his territories was broken, he returned to fight for his hereditary claim in 1189.

Reconciliation eventually followed in the typical feudal manner – through an arranged marriage. Henry's eldest son married Agnes, Barbarossa's niece and the Guelph and Ghibelline feud was thus brought to a close. Henry the Lion died in 1195, and was buried in Brunswick where his tomb still remains.

Oaths and Canonisation

One effect of the increasing difficulties with both papal and civil opposition was that Frederick and Rainald tried to draw the English King Henry II into imperial politics. They sent ambassadors to England to encourage marriage arrangements between two of Henry's daughters and Henry the Lion and one of Barbarossa's sons.

By Whitsun of 1165, Rainald had devised the Wuerzburg Oath. This important oath not only bound Barbarossa never to recognise Alexander as pope, but also bound imperial successors as well as the bishops and princes. Within six weeks all abbots, prelates and vassals were to take the oath. Refusal meant forfeiture of property, and exile. Freemen who failed to swear were to be mutilated and exiled.

On 29th December 1165, Charlemagne, the founder of the Holy Roman Empire, was canonised at Aachen. There had long been resistance to making him a saint due to his open contempt for Christian domestic morality (he had lived with concubines after the death of his last wife). But sufficient purgatorial time was deemed to have passed, and as far as Barbarossa was concerned, it was politically essential to state the unity of the empire and church by accepting Charlemagne into the body of saints at this time.

Revolt in Lombardy

In 1166 Barbarossa assembled his forces to return to Italy, where the rival Pope Alexander had fomented further rebellion. Frederick was determined to capture his papal enemy.

By the spring of 1167, northern Italy was divided between supporters of the empire – the Ghibellines – and defenders of civic independence – the Guelphs.

Barbarossa's imperial seal and signature of authority on a document dated July 1165.

Frederick put the rebellious cities under imperial ban, and intended to

Ratio suadet et iusticia exigit ut ad protectione et defensione ecclarum dei que per imperium nostrum longe lateque constitute sunt que nostre sola

cura extendam maxime quidem adillas a quibus orationum suffragia die ac nocte percipimus et si intabernaculo dei diligenter

aliquid superogauerimus abillo uero samaritano cum redierit nobis incentuplum esse reddendum speramus et credimus

Va preter cognoscant uniuersi fideles imperii per theutonicum imperium constitui presentes et futuri quod nos intuitu

diuine retributionis et pro nostra omniumque parentum nostrorum salute dilectum nostrum Geboldum venerabilem abbem

castellensem totamque eius ecclam monachos et fres ibidem deo seruientes familiam et omnia bona predicto monasterio

iuste pertinentia illa uidelicet que dilectus patruus noster heinricus dux austrie prefato monasterio libere contulit

et nominatim bona uille que alesbach uulgo dicitur et quecumque ne habet ut imposterum deo iuuante rationabiliter

acquirere poterit sub nostram imperialem tuicione ac defensione suscepimus Inde est quod nostra imperiali aucto

ritate statuentes precipimus ut nullus deceto epc nulla secularis persona uel ecclastica prefatum abbem uel ei fratres

siue bona eis pertinentia occasione alicui potestatis uel iusticie uiolenter aut iniuste molestare grauare uel

inquietare presumat Siquis aut hoc nostrum preceptum ausu temerario infringere presumpserit [...] p

pena conponat dimidiu fisco nostro et dimidiu predicto abbi et ei eccle hic tamen ut reu maiestatis nostre tadiu

esse se nouerit donec predictam conpositionem cum integritate persoluerit.

SIGNVM DOMNI FRIDERICI ROMANORVM IMPERATORIS INVICTISSIMI.

Ego Cristanus sacri palacii imperialis Cancellarii Recognoui.

Acta sunt hec Anno dnice Incarnationis mo co Lxv Indictione xiii

Regnante dno Frederico Romanorum Imperatore Victoriosissimo.

Anno Regni eius xiii Imperii uero xi feliciter Amen.

Dat Ratispone viiii Kalendas Julii.

finally suppress the opposition of Milan, Piacenza, Cremona, Mantua, Brescia, Parma, Bergamo and the March of Verona. The result was the formation of the Lombard League, made up of sixteen cities united against the empire. Their aim was to fight for full independence, and to restore Italy to the rights that had been established under Henry V, Lothar III and Barbarossa's immediate predecessor Conrad III.

Between 1168 and 1174, Barbarossa spent what is often termed the middle period of his reign in Germany. He considered some serious reversals of his policies, and declared his son Henry VI King of Germany and King of the Romans. Meanwhile, he attempted to settle the continuing conflict between Henry the Lion and his numerous opponents, which so weakened German unity.

By 1170 further negotiations with Pope Alexander, still in opposition to Frederick, had broken down. It was rumoured that Frederick had attempted to encourage Alexander to crown or at least support the coronation of his son Henry. In return, Henry (but not his father) would agree to recognise Alexander as rightful pope. When Frederick learned of the breakdown of negotiations, while at his court at Fulda in June of 1170, he solemnly repeated his oath never to recognise Alexander.

By 1174 Frederick had led yet another expedition into Italy. However, his princes were not enthusiastic about the project this time and his army was weak, so he was forced to hire roaming mercenaries. These *brabanzonen*, as they were known, were a growing social and political problem at this time and Alexander had even issued a decree forbidding their use. Frederick planned to attack Lombardy from the east and west simultaneously, perhaps remembering the renowned pincer campaigns for which Charlemagne had been famous.

Neither side, however, was particularly willing to enter into serious combat. By Easter of 1175 the Peace of Montebello was partly drawn up, although negotiations collapsed and the war recommenced.

German armour, typical of that worn by the Hohenstaufen knights, on a warrior of about 1100.

Third Plan – and Death

On 29th May 1176 Frederick was defeated at the battle of Lagnano because Henry the Lion, continually striving to increase his own power, had deserted the imperial cause at the last minute. But by 1177 Barbarossa had established the Peace of Venice, which brought agreement between Pope and Emperor. Alexander was escorted to Rome by Christian of Mainz, and Frederick's imperial power was recognised by the various factions.

But conflict with Henry the Lion soon became aggravated; Frederick acquired new territory in Saxony, Thuringia and Lusatia. Henry's failure

126

to attend and comply with imperial councils finally led to a declaration of forfeiture of his fiefs, and the title of Duke of Saxony was conferred upon Bernard of Anhalt, the younger of son of Albrecht the Bear.

In 1181 Pope Alexander died and was succeeded by Lucius III, who seemed willing to make compromises with Barbarossa.

By November of that year Henry the Lion had been defeated and banished from Germany for three years. This made it possible for Germany to develop economically and socially, and enabled Barbarossa to consolidate and extend his imperial and personal power throughout the German kingdom. Many new castles were built during this period, particularly in the north.

By May of 1184 Barbarossa was taking further steps against southern Italy, consolidating his hold by negotiation with the new pope, Lucius III. Then Henry VI, Barbarossa's son, and Constance of Sicily were formally engaged, an important dynastic move.

Just as Frederick was gaining increasing power in Italy, and it seemed that the Holy See would become isolated from general support, Lucius died in November of 1185 and the new Pope Urban III, was one of Barbarossa's fiercest opponents. When the marriage of Henry and Constance was solemnised on 27th January 1186, the ceremony was carried out by the Patriarch of Aquileia, who also crowned Henry as

Hohenstaufen castles had strong, cylindrical keeps, as at Muenzenberg in Hessen.

127

King of Italy. This was a direct challenge to Urban, who had not been consulted or even properly informed. A further period of imperial and papal conflict seemed likely.

But by 1187 Urban had died at Ferrara, and within two months, his successor Gregory VIII also died, at Pisa, while on his way to a meeting with Barbarossa. The next pope, Clement III, soon issued a solemn appeal for a crusade. Furthermore, he made real attempts to come to terms with the Emperor, and it seemed likely that the papal imperial conflict would now be resolved.

By March of 1188, Frederick seemed finally to have defeated his opponents on the major domestic and imperial fronts. In the summer he made his last will, and assembled a vast army to take Jerusalem from the great Saracen leader Saladin.

Jerusalem and Death

In May of 1189 an army of 20,000 men was assembled at Ratisbon. It was the largest force that Barbarossa had ever led, and was made up of experienced warriors, loyal princes and vassals, the epitome of the feudal army under its divinely appointed emperor. On 11th May, the many battalions, each comprising 500 men, left Ratisbon in great pomp and splendour.

Frederick first led the army successfully into Syria, and took the city of Iconium. He then moved on into Armenia, but on 10th June 1190, while

During six Italian campaigns, Barbarossa mercilessly razed several cities, including powerful Milan whose population was deliberately dispersed. German foot soldiers acted as engineers, demolishing walls and buildings.

crossing the River Salef, his horse shied suddenly and Barbarossa fell and disappeared beneath the swiftly flowing waters. His lifeless body was eventually taken from the river.

Thus, while at the peak of his long and difficult reign, and while engaged upon an ideal cause that represented all that he stood for in terms of imperial and religious aims, Frederick Barbarossa probably died from what we would now recognise as a massive heart failure. Despite his arrogance and cruelty towards opponents, he had been a remarkably enlightened and often liberal and generous ruler. Perhaps it is not surprising that he became the subject of legend, his noble image inspiring the collective imagination to attach magical tales to his historical person.

Aftermath

The drowning of Barbarossa was a terrible blow to his immediate followers, and to Germany as a whole. A small party of his vassals took his body to nearby Antioch, where he was buried in the cathedral.

It may be difficult for the modern reader to grasp the emotional effect of his passing upon his people. Such a sudden death, while engaged upon a religious war, and without the essential last sacrament, seemed almost to be an impossibility, an event which flew in the face of all religion, order and concepts of essential rightness. What of his soul? Would he go to heaven, as he had been engaged upon a holy war, or would his sins, unforgiven, weigh against him? These questions were utterly demoralising to the vassals of the late Emperor, and were to cause debate and confusion for many years to come.

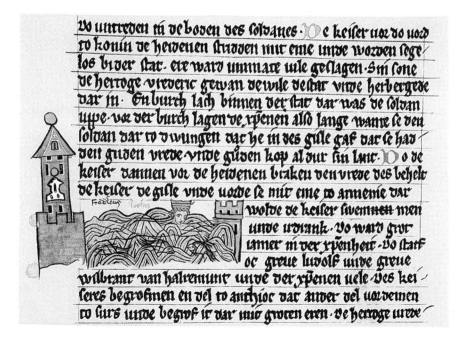

Barbarossa's death by drowning as described around 1250 in the Gotha manuscript of the Saxon Chronicle.

Barbarossa died by drowning or from a heart attack, falling from his horse while crossing the River Salef near Antioch. His sudden death, on the Third Crusade, devastated imperial morale, both political and religious.

The remains of Barbarossa's imperial palace at Gelnhausen.

Consequently, after Frederick's burial, some of his followers were so devastated that they committed suicide. Others, and this is most telling in the religious context, abandoned Christianity and became Muslims. They felt that with the Emperor's death, their Christian God had deserted them, or had proven incomprehensibly capricious; or more positively they felt that Allah suddenly was shown to be more powerful and in the right.

A body of men under Duke Frederick of Swabia proceeded to Acre to lay siege as planned, but the effort was half-hearted, and the arrival in strength of English and French forces by sea removed the Germans from the forefront of the crusade. Duke Frederick died of disease soon after.

The Succession

Before leaving for the crusade, Barbarossa had installed his son Henry as regent and upon hearing the news of his father's death, Henry succeeded to the imperial throne. However, his reign was to be a short one, for in 1191 he contracted a serious illness, and six years later he died.

Henry VI was not of the same calibre as his father. He blindly pursued established policies and fought to preserve his heritage of power, making little attempt to formulate new policies, and often taking cruel measures to enforce those already in existence. As with the reign of Charlemagne some 300 years earlier, we find that the death of a powerful and talented emperor takes the empire into the shadows also.

Following the proposals outlined in Barbarossa's third plan, Henry VI attempted to make the monarchy entirely hereditary, doing away with the elective powers of the princes. Despite offering similar hereditary rights to the nobles themslves, Henry was not successful in implementing this plan, but he died before any firm rejection of his proposals was made by the German princes. His only son was an infant, and his brother Phillip had to face a claim to the crown by Otto, son of Henry the Lion. Thus, Frederick II, grandson of Frederick Barbarossa, ruled in Sicily and fought to extend his power into northern Italy, but never ruled in Germany in the manner of his illustrious forebear. The final blow to Barbarossa's original plan to restore the Holy Roman Empire, extend it, and give the emperor equal or superior rights to the pope, came when Innocent III became pope. After the death of Henry VI, Innocent took advantage of the continuing civil war in Germany to undo any of the advances that Frederick Barbarossa had gained over the papal power. Although legend persisted regarding Barbarossa, by the beginning of the thirteenth century, within a decade of his death, his historical achievements had virtually vanished.

The Sleeping Emperor

Some time after the death of Barbarossa, various legends became associated with his name. There is some evidence that these were originally connected to his grandson Frederick II, and that by the

Legendary in concept, this depiction of Barbarossa at Gelnhausen portrays him in the company of mythical beasts.

mysterious process of collective imagination and tradition, they became drawn to the more powerful figure of Barbarossa.

What is certain is that he carried the legend of a king or emperor waiting to be reborn for several centuries, just as the British King Arthur has done. We may consider this legend on three levels: nationalistic, poetic or dreamlike, and mythical.

The first level is the most obvious: the sleeping Barbarossa and his knights represent that upsurge of Germanic nationalism and imperialism which occurs in every century. In this sense he is symbolic of the nationalistic cause, either to restore Germany to her former glories, or to justify and inspire territorial ambitions. Within folklore it is always the first theme, that of restoration, which occurs. The more political and propagandist elements are absent from tradition.

The second level, that of poetic or dream symbolism, is inherent in all folk-tales, traditions and motifs of regeneration. Here Barbarossa represents the redress of wrongs, the cure of ills, the great king who will return to bring a new golden age. This leads in turn to the third and deepest level of the motif, the mythical aspect. In this last context we find, curiously, the most ancient and primal root of the entire theme of the sleeping king. He is a representation or manifestation of the Titan Cronos, giant ruler of a distant Golden Age and paradisal land, said to be sleeping in the Otherworld, awaiting a final time of awakening.

Quite why this theme should be attached to Barbarossa in particular is not immediately clear; it would be equally valid, and perhaps more apt, if it were told of Charlemagne. Perhaps it was attached to the great Frankish emperor originally, for one variant of the tale names the sleeping king as 'Charles'. It may be that the curiosity of Frederick I having a red beard has caused him to remain in the popular imagination: red-headed men and women have many superstitions attached to them, particularly red-headed kings.

Those then are the general themes of Barbarossa as a legendary character. The following four German folktales relating to this theme, as collected by the Grimm brothers in the nineteenth century, are typical but only a fraction of the many variants known.

The Missing Emperor

The Emperor Frederick was excommunicated by the Pope; he was not allowed to enter churches and no priest would celebrate Mass for him. Just before Easter, when everyone was preparing to celebrate the great festival, the emperor went out hunting to be away from the festivity. Nobody knew what was really in his heart and mind.

He put on exquisite robes that had come as a gift from distant India, and took of vial of scented water, then mounted upon his noble steed. Only a small number of men accompanied him into the forest. Suddenly, he held up a wondrous ring upon his finger, and vanished from sight.

The Emperor was never seen again. Where he went, if he lost his life in the forest, if he was ripped apart by savage beasts, or if he was still alive, no one knew. Yet old farmers say that Frederick does still live, and that he occasionally appears disguised as a pilgrim. Furthermore, he proclaimed that he would one day rule again over the Roman Empire, that he would vex dishonest priests, and that he would not cease from battle until the Holy Land was delivered into Christian hands. Only then would he hang the burden of his shield upon a withered branch.

Barbarossa in Mount Kyffhausen

Many legends are told of Barbarossa; it is said that he is not dead, that no true Emperor has ruled since his reign, and that he lives on until the Day of Judgement. Until that time, he will remain hidden in Mount Kyffhausen. When he finally emerges, he will hang his shield on a leafless tree, which will sprout green leaves, and a better age will begin.

Occasionally, he talks to people who enter the mountain, though at other times he can be encountered outside. He usually sits upon a bench at a round stone table, resting his head in his hands, sleeping. He nods his head and blinks his eyes with sleep. His red beard has grown very long, right through the stone table; when it has encircled the table three times it will be the time of awakening. It has now circled the stone table twice.

In the year 1669, a peasant was taking grain from Reblingen to Nordhausen. Along the route he was stopped by a dwarf and led into the mountain, where he was told to empty his grain sacks and fill them with gold. He saw Barbarossa sitting there motionless.

Also a shepherd, who was whistling a tune that the emperor liked, was led into the mountain by a dwarf. The emperor rose as he approached and asked him 'Are the ravens still flying around the mountain?' The shepherd answered that they were, and the emperor cried 'Now I am going to have to sleep for another hundred years!'

The Shepherd on Mount Kyffhausen

Many people say that near Frankenhausen in Thuringia is a mountain in which Frederick Barbarossa may be found . . . he has been seen there many times.

A shepherd who kept his flock upon the side of the mountain and knew the legend, began one day to play upon his bagpipes. When he thought that he had fulfilled his duty well, he called out in a loud voice: 'Emperor Frederick this tune is presented to you!' The Emperor suddenly appeared and said 'May God greet thee, little man. May I ask in whose honour you were playing those pipes?'

'I played for Emperor Frederick', answered the shepherd.

'If thou hast done so', said the Emperor, 'Come with me, and thou wilt be rewarded for thy playing'.

Relief carving of Barbarossa as Emperor, in the cloisters of St Zeno Convent.

'But I dare not leave my sheep', cried the shepherd. 'Follow me and no harm will come to thy sheep', the Emperor replied, and taking him by the hand led him into a cave in the side of the mountain. They came to an iron door that immediately opened onto a marvellous hall where many servants paid honour to the shepherd.

Emperor Frederick showed him great kindness and asked what reward he wanted for playing so well upon the bagpipes. The shepherd replied 'None'.

'Go', said Barbarossa, 'And take one of the supporting feet from my golden cask as your payment'. The shepherd did as he was ordered, and was ready to leave, when the Emperor started showing him many wondrous weapons, armour, swords, and muskets. He told the shepherd to tell his own people that he would use these weapons to regain the Holy Sepulchre. Then he allowed his guest to leave.

The following day the shepherd took the golden cask foot to a goldsmith, who confirmed that it was genuine gold and bought it immediately.

Barbarossa in Kaiserslautern

Many people claim that Frederick was imprisoned by the Turks, and that

after his release he returned to Kaiserslautern and lived there for a long time. He is said to have built his palace next to a beautiful lake, now called Emperor's Lake. He is also said to have caught a huge carp there, and to commemorate this event he took a gold ring from his finger and wore it ever after as an earring. It is believed that this giant carp is still within the lake, and will not be caught until Frederick reigns again.

When people still fished in the lake two carp were caught joined together with golden chain around their necks. This event has been carved on Metzler Gate in Kaiserslautern for as long as people can remember.

Not far from the palace a fine zoological garden was built so that the Emperor could view all kinds of wonderful animals from his window. It has long since been turned into a pond and moat.

Frederick's bed is said to be still in the palace, hanging from iron chains. Although this bed is neatly made in the evenings, it is found disturbed again every morning, as if someone sleeps in it each night.

There is a cliff in Kaiserslautern which holds a cave so deep and mysterious that no one has discovered its bottom. Tradition says that Emperor Frederick, who was missing, lives there. A man once attempted to descend into the cave on a long rope tied at the surface to a bell. He could ring the bell when he could descend no further. Reaching the bottom he saw the Emperor Frederick with a long beard, sitting on a golden throne. The Emperor spoke to him and said that as long as he did not speak to anyone in that underground place, nothing would happen to him. He should also tell his master whatever he had seen. The adventurer looked about him, and saw a wide beautiful lawn on which many people stood around the Emperor. Finally, he rang his bell and was pulled up unharmed to the surface, where he delivered the emperor's words to his master.

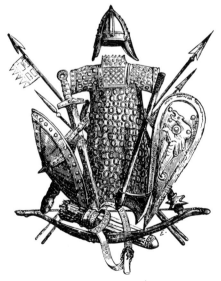

Barbarossa's Letter to Otto, Bishop of Freising (1157)

Frederick, by God's grace emperor of the Romans august forever, sends his regards and every good wish to his beloved uncle Otto, Bishop of Freising.

We have received with great joy the Chronicle, sent to us through your love, which you in your wisdom have complied, or rather brought into harmony things obscured by neglect. [This was the chronicle known as *The Two Cities* written by Otto between 1143 and 1147].

After the sweat of war we ardently desire to occasionally delight ourselves therein and be instructed in the virtues by the magnificent achievements of the emperors. But we would be pleased to commend to your attention an account, briefly compiled according to your own request, of the deeds performed by us since coming to the throne, save that by comparision to former deeds accomplished by better men they may be called the shadow rather than the reality of events. However, since your brilliant mental powers can exalt that which is insignificant and write greatly from small materials, we put more confidence in your praises than in our personal merits, and undertake to outline what little we have done in the Roman world during the past five years.

After we were anointed at Aachen, receiving the crown of the German realm, we held a general assembly at Merseburg on Whitsunday. There the Danish King Peter came as summoned to our assembly, and after pledging allegiance and fealty to us, received the crown of his realm from our hands.

Then we transferred Wichmann bishop of Zeitz to the archbishopric of Magdeburg; and though many disputes and arguments between ourself and the Roman Church resulted from this act, finally apostolic authority confirmed our laudable decision.

After this we commenced our Roman expedition and entered Lombardy in force. Because this land, due to the long absence of the emperors, had become proud, and, knowing its strength and becoming rebellious, we were angry and destroyed most of its strongholds not by the just and righteous wrath of our knights, but by the lower ranks.

The cunning and proud Milanese swore falsely to us promising much money, if we would grant them lordship over Como and Lodi. But as they could persuade us neither by praise or bribery, upon our arrival in their land they forsook their own fruitful country and led us for three days in the wilderness until finally, in opposition to their desires, we pitched camp about one German mile from Milan itself. As we demanded supplies for the army and they refused to furnish such supplies, we had their finest fortress, Rosate, which held five hundred armed men, taken and destroyed by fire. After this our soldiers advanced to the gate of Milan and wounded many and took large numbers of captives. With hostilities ensuing generally, we crossed the river Ticino near Novara and took forced possession of two bridges defended by towers. After our entire army had crossed, we had these bridges destroyed. Next we destroyed three of their strongest fortresses, namely, Momo, Galliate, and Trecate. After celebrating the birthday of our Lord with great joy, we marched through Vercelli and Turin and crossed the river Po.

We next destroyed Chieri, which was a large and well fortified town. We laid waste the city of Asti by fire. Then we besieged Tortona, a city superbly fortified by both art and nature. After three days we reduced the outer fortifications and might have captured the citadel itself, had not nightfall and a severe storm prevented us. Finally, after many assaults, much bloodshed, lamentable slaughter of our foes, and great losses to our own men, the city capitulated; we freed a certain leader of the Greeks who had been taken captive by Marchese Malaspina.

When Tortona was finally destroyed, the people of Pavia requested us to their city to give us a glorious triumph after the victory. We spent three days there, wearing the crown and receiving the maximum acclaim and respect of the populace. Then we advanced straight through Lombardy, Romagna, and Tuscany, and so reached Sutri. There the lord Pope, with the complete Roman Church, met us with joy, paternally offered us holy consecration, and complained to us of the injuries which he had suffered at the hands of the Roman people.

So we came to Rome, advancing daily together, lodging together, and exchanging genial conversation. The Romans sent messengers to us demanding a huge sum of money in exchange for their loyalty and submission, and also three sworn guarantees. Therefore we took counsel with the lord Pope and his cardinals. Since we were unwilling to buy the imperial title and were under no obligation to swear oaths to the rabble, in order to evade their treachery and stratagems the greater portion of our army, under the guidance of Cardinal Octavian, entered by night through a small gate near St Peter's, and so had already occupied the monastery of St Peter when we arrived.

When day dawned, the lord Pope and the entire church preceded us to the Basilica of St Peter and bade us welcome with a magnificent procession beginning at the steps. After celebrating Mass at the altar of Peter and Paul in honour of the Holy Virgin Mary, for it was Sunday, the Pope lavishly bestowed upon my head the blessing of the crown and of the Roman empire. After this had been duly carried out, while we returned to our camp exhausted by the effort and the heat and were taking food, the Roman people dashed forth from the Tiber bridge attempting to capture the Pope in the monastery of St Peter, and killing two of our servants and despoiling the cardinals.

We heard the uproar from our position beyond the walls, and hastened fully armed into the city. All that day we fought the Romans, killing almost a thousand of them and throwing them into the River Tiber, leading off captives, until night finally separated us from them.

When day dawned, our food supplies had failed, so we withdrew, taking with us the pope and cardinals, rejoicing in triumph over our victory. After all the fortifications around the City had surrendered to us, we came to Albano and remained there with the Pope for several days. From there we travelled to Spoleto, and because of its defiance in holding captive Count Guido Guarra and our other messengers, we assaulted that city. The judgement of God is marvellous and inscrutable! Fighting from the third to the ninth hour of the day, we took by storm, which is, by fire and sword, this most strongly fortified of cities with almost a hundred towers. After plundering booty beyond measure and burning even more in the flames, we utterly razed the city.

Turning from there to Ancona, we met with Palaelogus, the noble Greek prince, and Maroducas his associate, with other envoys from Constantinople. They solemnly vowed to us an enormous sum of money as incitement to enter Apulia and undertake by our might and power the downfall of William, who was enemy to both empires. But our army had been much weakened by its many hardships and campaigns, and our leaders decided to return home rather than go down into Apulia.

As we were returning and the Greek forces were advancing into Apulia, self-confident in their numbers and rich treasure, Palaelogus died after taking Bari and razing its fortifications. William collected an army, and made a sudden attack upon the Greeks, taking a few captive, killing all the rest, and carrying off all the treasure. But we arrived safely at Verona with a great victory offered us by God – such a victory as we have never before heard of being gained by only eighteen hundred soldiers. How they laid a trap for us on the steep slopes of a certain mountain, and how they were slain by us and twelve of them hanged, you have already heard. Furthermore, you know in turn the accord we made between your own brother the duke of Austria, and the duke of Bavaria, and how gloriously we elevated Frederick to the archbishopric of Cologne.

These few events, set forth in brief words, we offer to your famous skill to be amplified and enhanced.

Papal Allegiances

(Major figures are indicated in **bold** type)

Eugenius III *dies 8.7.1153* pro-imperial
Anastasius IV *dies 3.12.1154* pro-imperial
Hadrian (Nicolas Brakespear) *1154–1159 dies 1.9.1159* anti-imperial
Victor (Octavian) *1159–1164 dies April 1164* pro-imperial
Alexander III (Roland) *1159–1181 (in exile)* anti-imperial
Paschal III (Guido of Cremo) *1164 (the 'anti-pope')* pro-imperial
Kalixt III *1168–1178* pro-imperial
Innozenz III *1179–1180* pro-imperial
Lucius III *1181–1185*
Urban III (Uberto Crivelli) *1185–1187* strongly anti-imperial
Gregor VIII *1187*
Clemens *1187–1191*

Barbarossa was crowned Emperor Frederick I by the Pope. Despite their spiritual office, medieval popes were totally involved in secular politics, holding court in costume and pontifical regalia which expressed their great power.

Cologne Cathedral today. This great medieval church still holds the shrine of the Three Wise Men, taken there by Barbarossa's Chancellor Rainald von Dassell.

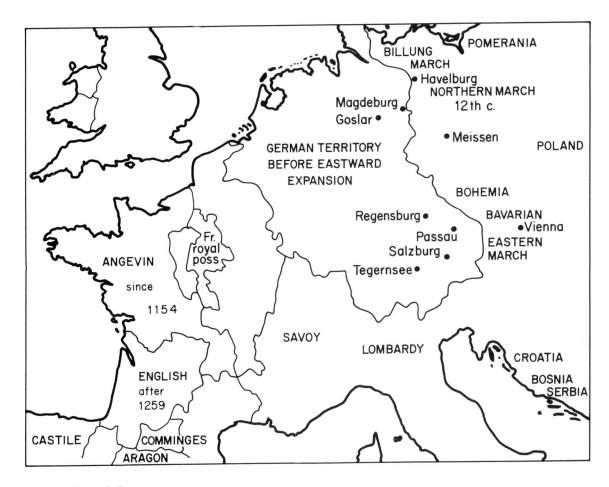

Western and central Europe from the twelfth to thirteenth centuries.

Bibliography

Baeuml, F.H. *Medieval Civilization in Germany 800–1273* Thames & Hudson, London, 1969.

Bishop, M. *The Penguin Book of the Middle Ages* Penguin, Harmondsworth, 1971.

Brooke, C. *The Structure of Medieval Society* Thames & Hudson, London, 1971.

Freising, Otto of *The Deeds of Frederick Barbarossa* Columbia University Press, New York, 1953.

Frenzel, H.A.U.E. *Daten Deutscher Dichtung* Vol.I Deutscher Taschenbuch Verlag, München, 1962.

Hay, D. *The Medieval Centuries* Methuen, London, 1953.

Munz, P. *Frederick Barbarossa, A Study in Medieval Politics* Eyre & Spottiswoode, London, 1969.

Pacaut, M. *Frederick Barbarossa* Collins, London, 1970.

Rowling, M. *Everyday Life in Medieval Times* Batsford, London, 1968.

Treharne, R.F. & H. Fullard *Muir's Atlas of Ancient, Medieval and Modern History* George Philip, London, 1982.

Ward, D. *The German Legends of the Brothers Grimm* Vols. I and II Millington, London, 1981.

GENEALOGY OF CHARACTERS

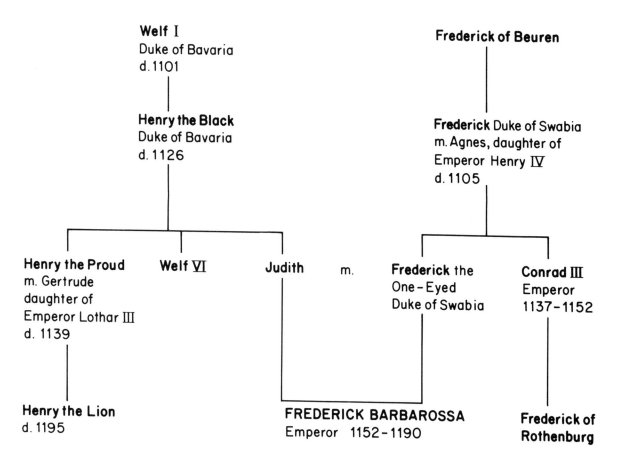

Richard Lionheart

THE CRUSADER KING

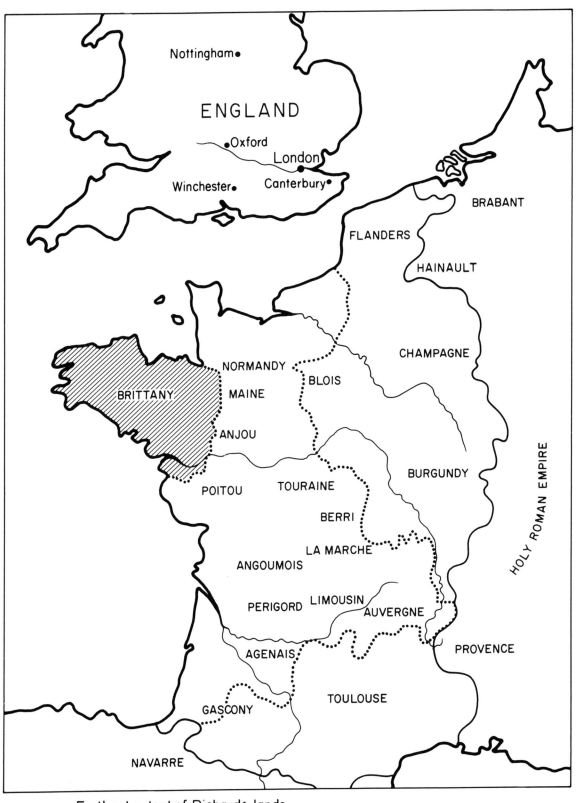

Nottingham

ENGLAND

Oxford
London
Winchester
Canterbury

BRABANT

FLANDERS

HAINAULT

CHAMPAGNE

NORMANDY
BLOIS
MAINE
BRITTANY
ANJOU
BURGUNDY
POITOU
TOURAINE
BERRI
LA MARCHE
ANGOUMOIS
PERIGORD
LIMOUSIN
AUVERGNE
PROVENCE
AGENAIS
TOULOUSE
GASCONY

HOLY ROMAN EMPIRE

NAVARRE

•••••••••••• Furthest extent of Richards lands

I knew the man, my dear master and a great king, who brought the leopards into the shield of England . . . Of him therefore . . . the hymned and reviled, the loved and loathed, spendthrift and miser, king and beggar . . . of King Richard Yea-and-Nay, so made, so called, I thus prepare my account.

(*The Life and Death of Richard Yea-and-Nay* Maurice Hewlett)

The Young Lion

The image that most people have of Richard I *Coeur de Lion* is of a brave, chivalrous knight and a fearless soldier. At times he attains almost mythical stature, appearing in the ballad cycles of Robin Hood as a noble saviour contrasted to bad King John.

The reality is somewhat different. Richard certainly was brave, and undoubtedly he was a good soldier. But he was also boorish, sadistic and greedy, once personally overseeing the execution of 2,500 Moslem prisoners. He preferred the furtherance of his own prestige over the needs of his kingdom – especially England, from where he was absent for almost the entire period of his kingship.

Historians are divided over Richard's abilities as a king. To some he was wholly bad, to others merely indifferent. Few find him more than adequate and even fewer describe him as good or even satisfactory. He knew no English and took no interest in what he must have regarded as a farflung outpost of his Angevin Empire – except for the revenues it could bring. Thus, the nineteenth century historian Bishop Stubbs said that Richard 'Was a bad king . . . his ambition that of a mere warrior. He would fight for anything whatever, but he would sell everything that was worth fighting for.'

Born on 8th September 1157 at Oxford, Richard's early days were totally overshadowed by his remarkable parents. King Henry II was wily, ambitious, and possessed of one of the keenest minds in Christendom. His mother, Eleanor of Aquitaine, was beautiful, vengeful and intellectually the equal of any man. They are two of the most colourful and exciting figures in the whole of medieval history. Being their son must have meant living constantly in the shadow of two brilliant luminaries. Henry was an exacting master, possessed of so much energy that it was popularly rumoured that he could fly, so swiftly did he travel from place to place. Eleanor became the centre of the world of troubadour song and romance, the world of knights and ladies, of adventure, love and the wanderings of brave men in search of noble deeds. Small wonder if their son grew up with a taste for chivalrous pursuits, warlike deeds and sometimes foolhardy enterprise.

Unlike his father, Richard was no statesman. His ability to upset people and drive wedges between himself and those who were supposed to be his allies was famous. One such affront, to the Archduke of Austria, later cost him his freedom and caused him to suffer a long imprisonment from which he was only freed at huge expense – much of which was raised by his neglected kingdom of England.

A Family of Conflict

Richard was brought up in France at his mother's court at Poitou. Eleanor and Henry had separated unofficially and there was no love lost between them. Richard was parcelled out to his mother, just as their other sons, Henry, Geoffrey and John, were kept by their father. Perhaps Richard had the best of it: at Queen Eleanor's court he encountered troubadours and intellectuals who taught him the social graces. In addition, he was able to take part in furious knockabout tournaments (Henry had banned them in England, deeming them a threat to public order) and this early training stood Richard in good stead in later life.

Certainly, there was nothing peaceful in the relationships between either the brothers or their father. In a chamber of the palace of Winchester, a fresco depicted an eagle being attacked by its fledglings. This was designed by Henry II himself in token of the way in which his own offspring spent most of their lives fighting against him. A strong man himself, Henry bred strong sons for whom even the great Angevin Empire was too small. For years the family spent most of their time in internecine struggle.

The reasons for this constant conflict are not hard to fathom. In 1170, Henry's eldest son was crowned by the Archbishop of York and was henceforward called 'the Young King' Henry. Richard, as second son, had been promised Aquitaine by his mother and had done homage to Louis VII of France. Geoffrey, the third son, was to marry the heiress to the Dukedom of Brittany. Between them the three sons held title to most of Henry II's kingdom – but title only. Henry II was barely thirty years of age and in the prime of his life. It would be a long time before anyone inherited – and his sons knew that sooner or later Henry would take something from them to give to the youngest of them all, John.

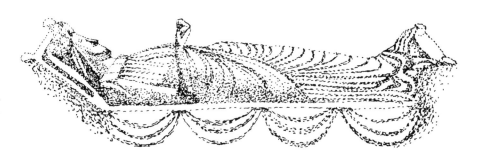

Tomb effigies of Eleanor of Aquitaine and of Henry II (opposite) from Fontrevault Abbey.

146

The upshot was that Richard, Geoffrey and the Young King Henry went to the court of the French King. From there they began formulating plans to take what they saw as rightly theirs, without waiting for their father's demise. Eleanor, disguising herself as a man, attempted to join them, but was captured and spent the rest of Henry II's reign in prison.

It was a strange situation, which must have made a lasting impression on Richard, who was more than usually close to his mother. Perhaps because of this he contrived to fight on even after his brothers had surrendered to the Old King. Finally, he too was forced to submit by Henry's superior forces and greater supply of money. Rather than punish him for the attempted rebellion, Henry gave Richard the task of quelling the very Aquitainian rebels from whom he had so recently looked for support.

It is typical of Richard that he accepted the task with alacrity and succeeded with such brilliance that almost overnight he became recognized as a famous warrior.

This did not please his elder brother, the Young King, who demanded that both Richard and Geoffrey should swear formal allegiance to him. This Henry almost persuaded them to do – until the Young King also demanded that Richard should swear his oath on a holy relic; at which Richard simply turned round and declared that Aquitaine was his anyway by right from his mother and had nothing to do with anyone else.

This so angered Henry II that he ordered his other sons to curb Richard's pride. Then, when both sides began to raise armies, he attempted to call a halt before civil war divided the Angevin Empire in half. In the end, by a touch of irony, the older Henry fought side by side with Richard against the other two brothers, thus reversing the roles of the earlier rebellion and causing the new French King, Philip II, to await the outcome with interest.

Then everything changed. In June 1183, the Young King fell victim to a sudden attack of dysentery and died a few days later. Richard was now heir to the throne of the Angevin Empire.

Henry II now hoped that things would settle down, and suggested that Richard should hand over Aquitaine to John, the youngest son. This

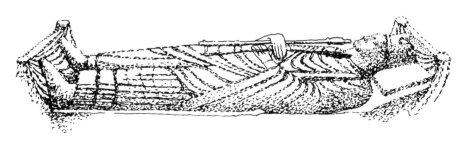

Richard refused to do, and once again the family brawls began. They might have continued unabated until Henry II's death, but two important factors altered the stakes for all the players in this complex game of dynastic skulduggery. First, only three years after the death of the Young King, Geoffrey, heir to Brittany, died in a tournament, leaving Richard and John as the only brothers to continue the struggle. The second factor was the appearance on the scene of a common enemy – though not immediately recognized as such. This was Philip II of France, whose extravagant plans for the future of his kingdom included the destruction of the Angevin Empire. Wooing first John and then Richard, Philip succeeded in keeping them at each other's throats, or at Henry's coat-tails, for several more years. Then, in 1187 an event occurred which was to change not only Richard's life, but the history of Europe and much of the rest of the world for generations to come.

Epoch of Change – Twelfth Century Europe

The twelfth century was an extraordinary period in many ways. It saw the laying to rest of the old war-torn, Dark-age Europe and the emergence of a distinct and purposeful civilization, which we now recognize as the first flowering of the Middle Ages. With the establishment of strong dynasties, civil wars and baronial insurrections were quelled or kept under control. European population began to expand in the more settled times. It was the time for the dissemination and transcription of stories and songs by means of travelling storytellers and poets; many of these, like Chrétien de Troyes and certain trouvères and troubadours received royal patronage. Stories of the great heroic kings like Arthur and Charlemagne were on everyone's tongue.

Crusades against Islam

Medieval North European civilization was to some extent an insular entity, shielded from its own past and from an encroaching future. Christianity had formalized society, bringing a standardization to culture, learning and administration. The Christianization of the rest of Europe and Russia was steadily progressing, though the fragmentation of the Christian church into Catholic West and Orthodox East was of recent origin: one clause of the creed – that the Holy Spirit proceeded from the Father 'and from the Son' (*filioque*) – had caused the Pope of Rome and the Patriarch of Byzantium to bombard each other with bulls and writs of excommunication. The West upheld the *filioque* clause; the East did not. And so the mutual help and support which should have

The Second Great Seal of Richard I, which shows him seated between the Moon and the Sun and bearing the symbols of his sovereignty.

typified Christian brothers became a stick which the Western church used in the coming crusade to beat Orthodox and infidel alike.

The idea of holy war (*jihad*) was native to Islam, a method of Moslem expansionism, but it was in Spain that Christianity first borrowed this notion. Roland's stand at Roncevalles against the Moslem army and El Cid's long campaign against the Moorish occupation of Spain vaunted the virtuous defence of Christendom. The feats of both heroes were the stuff of epic song. And so, when Byzantine emperor Alexius I appealed to Pope Urban II for help against the Seljuk Turks in Asia Minor, Urban saw the chance to vindicate the Western Church and show himself magnanimous to his Orthodox brothers. He sent the call through Europe to mobilize all Christian kings to liberate Jerusalem and the Holy Sepulchre. Jerusalem had been in Arab hands since the seventh century and the Holy Sepulchre was empty, but such was the emotional fervour stirred up by Urban's preachers that the First Crusade was launched and a new kind of 'holy war' was under way.

The old dictum 'might is right' which had typified the early years of the second millennium, was transformed to 'might *for* right'. Instead of fighting each other and laying waste Europe, crusading-spirited warriors now had licence to fight Moslems and plunder the infidels' land. The times were such that Christianity, whose founder taught brotherly love and forebearance, was quite incapable of applying these precepts within its own jurisdiction. The lesser evil was to syphon off the unschooled violence which was wrecking Europe and to apply it usefully elsewhere. It was in this early training ground that Britain discovered its propensity for colonization and love of Empire.

Despite their natural animosity, Christians and Moslems learned much from each other. Among the most famous of these cultural exchanges was chess, which was introduced into Spain during the tenth century. This reproduction from a thirteenth century chess manual shows a Christian and a Moslem playing a game.

Slaying Orthodox Christians, Jews and Moslems with great impartiality on their way, it took the crusaders two years to reach Jerusalem. There, many promptly claimed lands and titles and chose to remain. These men appreciated the riches of Islamic culture and technical achievement – and, doubtless, enjoyed the heady freedom of land without feudal obligations entailed to some ruthless overlord. It was these men who formed their own alliances and accommodations with Moslem rulers in exchange for peace. In contrast, the military orders like the Knights Templar undertook serious duties in protecting poor pilgrims from marauding bands of Moslems, as well as acting as an independent body of warrior-monks. The pattern of Europe was squarely placed upon the city of Jerusalem when, in 1100, Baldwin of Boulogne became the first King of Jerusalem. This was a political expediency which, in the later Middle Ages, was to become an empty if honourable title borne by otherwise undistinguished European rulers.

The Second Crusade was a less spectacular affair, failing because of many factors: the North German princes decided to direct their crusade against the pagan, Slavonic-speaking Wends; the French forces nearly attacked Constantinople as a result of severe relations between East and West; the native crusader barons were more determined to sustain their alliances with Moslem rulers in the Middle East than to help the next wave of crusaders (who might themselves claim lands).

Angevin Squabbles

While the Second Crusade was dragging on, Richard's father Henry II was consolidating his dynastic empire and England was in a state of civil war – which explains why no English king had yet appeared personally in the crusades.

Henry I of England, William the Conqueror's son, had left only one heir, Matilda, whom he had married to Henry V of Germany, the Holy Roman Emperor. At his death, Matilda's claim was overlooked in favour of Henry I's nephew, Stephen. There had ensued a formidable civil war, with the barons backing one side and then the other, while the Angevins undermined Stephen's kingship with carefully laid plans of their own.

Matilda's German husband had died in 1126. Henry I, her father, had ordered her back home to be used as a dynastic pawn. He rapidly re-established his alliance with the Angevin heir, Geoffrey, Duke of Anjou and Maine, by marrying him to his daughter. Matilda was still only 25 and Geoffrey a mere 14, but it was the wisest thing Henry I did in order to secure his dynastic survival (after the disastrous loss of his heir when the White Ship sank with loss of all hands, leaving him only a single female heir).

Geoffrey supported his wife's cause with vigour, but with two sets of lands to administer, Geoffrey attended to the French territories while

Geoffrey Plantagenet, Count of Anjou, as depicted in his tomb effigy.

Matilda went to uphold her claims to the queenship of England. The early life of their son, Henry II, was marked by the wrangle between Stephen and Matilda for the sovereignty of England. His succession to the English crown in 1154 at the age of 21 was hailed with relief by those worn down by insurrection and counter-bargaining. Anarchy was over and there now began the reign of one of the strongest kings ever to rule England, one whose territories and titles gave him authority over a great part of north-western Europe. He was count of Anjou in Maine after the death of his father; he was Duke of Normandy by right of his mother and Duke of Aquitaine by right of his wife, Eleanor, the divorced wife of King Louis VII of France. The only part of France which the French kings could claim as independent territory was restricted to north-eastern France and what is now Belgium. Such was the extent of the Angevin Empire. After decades of civil strife, Henry II was able to strengthen England and leave a vast domain to his sons – as previously described. The extent of the territory to be administered and the fact that Henry and Eleanor had four strong sons to inherit these lands was to prove a problem. For though Henry I had left England in a very confused state because he had only a daughter to inherit his title, Henry II's problem was quite the reverse.

With England once more stabilized, it could now afford to look beyond its own divisions and take a role in the affairs of Europe. Henry's

Armour and weapons from the First Crusade were closer in style to those of the Norman Conquest. A comparison with later styles shows the way in which armour developed in the years separating the first and third ventures into the Holy Land.

life-long role had been the Kingship of England, it was for his sons to look abroad for glory in battle.

Crusader King

Ever since the end of the First Crusade in 1100 and the unsuccessful conclusion of the Second in 1184, the tiny Christian Kingdom of Jerusalem – Outremer or the Land Beyond the Sea – had maintained a slender toehold on the eastern seaboard of the Holy Land. Surrounded on every side by the followers of Mohammed – who also laid claim to Jerusalem and its lands – it was only a matter of time before war broke out in earnest.

Then news reached Europe in 1187 of a great battle fought at Hattin, close to the Sea of Galilee. Here the Christian army, lead by Guy of Lusignan, the King of Jerusalem, had been utterly overwhelmed by a Moslem army lead by Al-Malik al-Nasir Salah ed-Din Yusuf, better known as Saladin. Guy was himself captured, and every surviving member of the two great military orders of the Templars and Hospitallers were executed. Jerusalem, the very heart of Christendom, had been captured and it could only be a matter of time before the remaining Christian forces, still holding on at Tyre, Tripoli and Antioch, were overcome or expelled.

A cry for help went out to Kings and Princes of the West, and Richard was one of the first to respond, receiving in November 1187 the piece of material cut into the shape of a cross which was the badge of all crusaders.

He did so without waiting for his father's permission. It was not until the end of the same year that Henry and Philip of France followed suit. Neither really wanted to take the Cross, being more concerned with their own affairs and plots against each other. However, public opinion and a gathering tide of religious fervour forced them to join their brother monarchs in swearing to raise armies to recapture the Holy City.

The rewards offered to those who did so were not inconsiderable. There were plenary indulgences, which meant the immediate forgiveness of all past sins and the promise of a place in heaven if they fell in battle. Also, on a more mundane level, there was the postponement of any financial debts then owing until such time as they returned from the crusade. This lead to numerous less-than-chivalrous characters joining the Christian armies for their own reasons. Yet there was also a genuine upsurge of religious feeling, of anger and hatred towards the infidels who had dared seize back the 'holy earth' so dearly bought with the blood of the First Crusade.

Mail hauberk of the kind worn by the crusaders in Richard's time.

152

Nonetheless, that inspired teacher Bernard of Clairvaux, who later on founded the Cistercian Order, knew well the innermost hearts of the army when he preached a sermon containing what must surely be the earliest ever advertising campaign:

O mighty soldier, O man of war, you now have a cause for which you can fight without endangering your soul . . . Or are you a shrewd business man, a man quick to see the profits of this world? If you are, I can offer you a splendid bargain. Don't miss this opportunity. Take the sign of the Cross . . . It doesn't cost much to buy and if you wear it with humility you will find it is worth the Kingdom of Heaven!

Stirred by thoughts of heroic deeds against the cruel and monstrous Saracens, Richard chafed, waiting for his father and Philip of France to settle their differences. Meetings between the two monarchs were arranged, but rather than bringing peace to the two countries, fresh hostilities broke out. Richard, alarmed that his father would appoint his younger brother as heir, tried to force Henry's hand by allying himself with Philip. In 1189 they invaded Maine and Henry, his tireless energy at last exhausted, fell ill. He withdrew to his favourite castle at Chinon and there, on 6th July he died, having learned at the last that his favourite son John had joined the rebels against him.

Richard was now King by right of birth and seniority. He visited his father's body where it lay in the abbey church of Fontrevault. Showing no emotion, he remained only a few minutes before turning away. It is said that as he left, blood flowed from the nostrils of the dead king, a fact which some took as a sign since the body of a murdered man will bleed in the presence of his murderer; but Henry's death was the outcome of a life lived at full tilt. Richard's only part was to hasten his father more quickly towards his end.

Richard I was crowned in England at Westminster on 3rd September 1189 and immediately set about raising money for the crusade. He sold castles, manors, privileges, public offices, even towns. He is said to have remarked: 'I would sell London, if I could find anyone rich enough to buy it.'

Finally, he sailed from Dover on 11th December 1189. Before he departed, he did his best to curb Prince John's ambition by giving him several huge tracts of English land in Derbyshire, Somerset, Dorset, Devon and Cornwall. At the same time, John was made Earl of Gloucester, and awarded the lands of Mortain in Normandy – to which he was instantly banished for a term of three years, Richard's clearest vote of no confidence in his brother.

The plan was for Richard and Philip to meet at Vézelay on 1st April 1190 and then to leave together for the Holy Land. Then news came that Philip's wife, Queen Isabel, had died suddenly. A further delay ensued and it was not until July that the two great armies finally set forth on the third anniversary of the Battle of Hattin. When Richard finally took up the scrip and staff of a pilgrim, the latter broke under him. Undeterred by

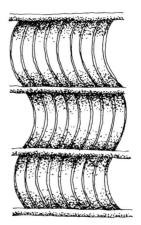

So-called 'banded mail' from which crusader armour was made. It could withstand all but point-blank arrows.

153

this ill omen, he set forth, intending to win not only fame and fortune but lands as well, which he had agreed to share equally with Philip. Their army has been estimated at between 6000 and 8000 men – a huge number for the time. It would be some four years before Richard saw England again. In the intervening time, he would become a changed man, as would many who set out with such high hopes to win back the holy earth of Outremer.

The Third Age

The helm of Richard Coeur de Lion.

The journey from Marseilles to the Holy Land should have taken fifteen days. It took Richard ten months; having set out filled with enthusiasm and burning ambition, the whole of the journey was fraught with disasters and setbacks.

At Lyons, the bridge over the Rhone collapsed from the weight of the men trying to cross – though fortunately only two were drowned. Richard had to organize a bridge of boats before he could cross. When he finally reached Marseilles, he expected to find the fleet of over a hundred ships which he had commissioned in advance. Instead, he found that they were still in Portugal, where their captains had become involved in the war against the Moors.

Furious, Richard hired thirty ships from the Marseilles merchants and set sail for Genoa, where Philip had arrived before him and promptly fallen ill. When the two kings met they had the first of many quarrels. Philip asked for the loan of five ships; Richard offered three. Philip refused and the stubborn men parted with harsh words.

Richard now pressed on to Salerno, where he wanted to discuss a recurrent ague with the city's famous doctors. There he learned that the original fleet was now in Sicily and he hastened on to Messina to join them.

He found Philip there before him and about to disembark. It seemed the two kings were trying to race each other to the Holy Land; certainly they wanted as little of each other's company as possible. Philip sailed but was forced to turn back almost at once by the weather. Once again, the two kings were stranded together at a time when the kingdom of Sicily was at a particularly explosive juncture in its long and turbulent history.

154

After the death of Sicily's most recent king, William II, a dispute arose over the succession, which should have gone to William's aunt; she was related to the son of the German Emperor, Frederick Barbarossa. This so alarmed the Sicilians, who wanted nothing to do with a German prince, that they gave the throne to William's illegitimate cousin, Tancred of Lecca, an ambitious man famed for his ugliness of both temper and physique.

The problem which arose when Richard's army arrived was caused by Tancred's withholding of a dowry promised to Richard's sister Joan – as well as the small matter of a legacy left by William II to Henry, who had been his father-in-law. Henry had died only a few weeks before William and this, so far as Tancred was concerned, meant that the arrangement was void. Of course, Richard disagreed and demanded payment in gold and ships for his army.

For a time, things hung in the balance, until Richard finally lost patience and took the city of Messina. This act was in opposition to Philip, who when the city had fallen, demanded that his own flag be raised over it, thus adding his own stake to any claim made upon Tancred.

Reluctantly, the Sicilian monarch paid up 20,000 ounces of gold for the unpaid dowry, and a further 20,000 ounces when Richard arranged a marriage between one of Tancred's daughters and his nephew and heir, Arthur of Brittany. In return, Richard promised military aid, if it should be needed, against the new German emperor. (Frederick Barbarossa had been drowned while his own crusading venture had barely started.)

By this time it was towards the end of October 1190 and too late to make the sea crossing to the Holy Land. Richard and Philip decided to

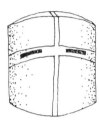

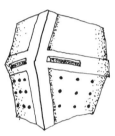

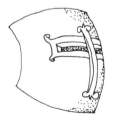

Helmets of the kind worn by the men who marched to the Holy Land with Richard.

winter in Sicily, and there celebrated Christmas in style, while the Christian forces across the sea suffered terrible privations from disease and starvation.

Also, while he was in Sicily, Richard heard that the current abbot of the monastery of Calabria, Joachim of Fiore, had announced a unique system of prophetic insight based upon Biblical references. According to this divination, there were three ages of mankind, the third of which – the Age of the Spirit – was about to dawn. This would be signified by the defeat of Saladin, whom Joachim saw as the current Antichrist.

Richard at once demanded to know when this would happen and was told 1194 (four years hence). 'Then,' said Richard, 'I have gone on crusade too soon.'

Joachim reassured him that he was needed and would have God on his side. Richard had to be satisfied with this response, but he was clearly convinced thereafter that he was destined to overcome Saladin.

Mediterranean Marriage

February of 1191 came and still Richard delayed. A fresh quarrel broke out between him and the King of France. Richard had been engaged to Philip's sister Alys since 1169. Suddenly, Eleanor of Aquitaine, seventy years old but as active as ever, arrived in Messina with a new bride for her son. Berengaria was the daughter of the King of Navarre and a good match for Richard – but Philip, needless to say, was furious. The argument raged for days, then Richard suddenly declared that he would not marry Alys because she had been his father's mistress and had borne him a son. This may or may not have been true, though knowing Henry II, it may well have been. Nevertheless, Richard declared that he had witnesses to prove it and Philip made a tactful withdrawal, secretly plotting with Tancred.

Richard, however, had already made overtures of friendship to the Sicilian king and cemented this by giving him a rich and generous gift – Excalibur, the magical sword of King Arthur. (Quite how he had come by this weapon, since it was cast into the lake at the conclusion of that great king's reign, is not recorded!)

By then, it was the season of Lent. Since he could not get married (marriages were never solemnized during Lent) Richard decided to delay no longer, Philip having sailed already. Also, Richard thought to have the marriage ceremony performed in the Holy Land. Thus, on 10th April 1191, he finally sailed from Sicily. His fleet is said to have numbered more than 200 vessels and his army had grown even larger since leaving France.

But he was still fated not to complete his voyage without problems. A storm blew up before they were three days out from Sicily, and several ships were either wrecked or blown off course. Among the latter was the ship carrying Berengaria and Richard's sister Joan.

Reaching the island of Rhodes, Richard decided to wait there while he sent fast ships in pursuit of the missing vessel. He soon learned that it had come ashore on the island of Cyprus, where the ruler, Isaac Ducas Comnenus, had already seized several survivors from other wrecks and now virtually held Richard's bride and his sister to ransom.

At once, Richard set forth for Cyprus and after unsuccessful negotiations with Isaac, laid siege to Limassol. He captured this easily and chased Isaac inland, having ensured the safety of Berengaria and Joan. At this juncture he received a visit from the leaders of the Christian forces in the Holy Land, who came to ask for his support against Philip of France. That wily monarch had reached Acre in April and at once began plotting to make himself King of Outremer, pushing the incumbent Guy of Lusignan off the throne.

Richard at once agreed to help in return for assistance in his immediate design, the conquest of Cyprus. He received the help he needed and in the next three months showed his superb generalship by totally subduing the island. He captured Isaac's wife and daughter, and having promised not to put the former ruler in irons, had silver chains made for him.

Richard now married Berengaria in a wedding long remembered for its splendour. He seems to have been content with his wife, though he saw little enough of her in the years which followed.

Kolossi Castle near Limassol, Cyprus. Richard landed here in 1191 in pursuit of his bride Berengaria. He conquered Cyprus in three months and established there a base of operations for the Christian forces in the East.

The Christian base on Cyprus was of immense strategic importance for the crusaders, who now had both a jumping-off point for their armies and a supply base which was virtually impregnable.

On 5th June, Richard finally set sail on the final leg of his long journey, reaching Tyre next day. Here the garrison, acting on advice from Philip, refused to admit him. Enraged, Richard sailed on and landed at Acre, joining the besieging army on 8th June.

For Richard, the Third Age foretold by Joachim of Fiore had now begun.

Weapons and Warfare

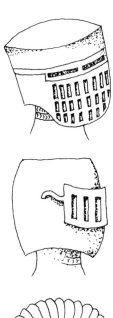

The period between the end of the twelfth century and the middle of the thirteenth saw several crucial innovations in weaponry and armour which helped make the medieval knight what he was always intended to be: a superb fighting machine.

Within a space of some twenty years, chain mail virtually replaced a variety of earlier forms of armour. Additionally, the development of the huge 'pot' helm, which enclosed all of the head rather than just the skull, made its wearer virtually invulnerable against anything less than a blow delivered with the full weight of a sword or axe.

We take chain mail very much for granted, seeing it depicted in paintings of the time, or in recent cinematic extravaganzas. Yet it was by no means easy to manufacture. We tend to forget the immense labour involved in forging the literally thousands of wire rings, which had then to be beaten flat, holes drilled into each end, and rivets added. For additional strength, mail coats were constructed from patches of four links to one. They were then further riveted, welded, or soldered and various parts strengthened even further by doubling or even trebling the rings.

Providing it was kept free from rust, a good coat of mail, made by a master armourer, would last its owner a lifetime. It was kept clean by the simple method of scrubbing it with fine sand – a commodity in no short supply during Richard's desert campaigns!

The helm evolved gradually from the conical Norman helmet, ear flaps being added. These flaps gradually grew larger until they met the nasal and became a single sheet of metal, with slits to allow vision and holes for breathing. These massive objects sometimes weighed several pounds, and with the addition of padding must have been unbearably hot. If we imagine the knight of Richard's time riding into battle with a padded gambeson (quilted body-armour), chain mail shirt and hose, topped by the huge helm, and swinging a heavy longsword – all in the blistering heat of the desert and against a much lighter-clad adversary –

Further examples of crusader helmets

we may wonder that the crusaders managed to win *any* battles. But these were superb fighting men, forged by the iron wills and driving energy of their leaders until they could master any terrain or circumstance.

Origins of Heraldry

With the development of the all-enclosing helm came a further necessity – that of recognition. It is generally accepted that during the period of the First Crusade knights began to wear distinguishing marks of one kind or another. Such marks were either on their shields, or in the form of an effigy attached to the top of the helm. Thus Richard himself is depicted on his Great Seal with a lion *passant* on the side of his helm, topped by a fan-shaped ornament.

A Spanish poet of the eleventh century describes how:

> Some of the knights placed upon their armour
> signs that were different one from another
> in order to be known thereby, while others
> placed them upon their heads, or on their horses.
> *(Lays de Partida)*

These distinguishing devices developed in time into the system we now know as heraldry.

Knight in crusader style of mailed hauberk and surcoat with helmet, shield and sword: from the effigy on the tomb of Lord Robert of Tattershall at Kirkstead in Lancashire.

Arms and Weaponry

The sword and mace were still favourite weapons for hand-to-hand fighting, though the famous charge of the Frankish knights with levelled lances was still an awesome and terrible thing to the lightly-armed Saracens.

Swords were about thirty inches in length, the blade two-edged and tapering towards a diamond-shaped point. The quillons were short at this time, curving slightly towards the blade, while the grip was short without a swell, the pommel being usually a simple knob or wheel-shape.

Richard is said to have favoured the axe as a hand-to-hand weapon, and a contemporary poem records that he had one made specially before departing for the Holy Land:

> Then King Richard I understond,
> Ere he went out of Engilond,
> Let make an axe for the nones
> Therewith to cleve the Saracens' bones.
> The head in sooth was wrought full weele,
> Thereon was twenty pounds of steele,
> And when he came to Cyprus londe
> This iron axe he took in honde.

Against this armoured might the Saracens had little or no defence save superior numbers and the horrors of heat and sickness. Their armour,

An axe-head from the period of the second Crusade.

though skilfully made and often beautiful, was far less durable than that of the crusaders. They had always relied on speed and skill in horsemanship, which enabled them to dash in upon their adversaries, fire off a salvo from their short but deadly bows, and then retreat before any reprisal.

But Saracen arrows did not have the power of penetration necessary to pierce the heavy mail hauberks of the Christian knights, and whenever their numbers were inferior they were frequently overwhelmed by the sheer weight and ferocity of their opponents.

Cavalry Tactics

The great hero Rodrigo del Bivar – El Cid – had been the first person to use the weight of heavily armed cavalry against the more lightly clad Moors. Richard and the Crusaders adopted this method of battle, countering the Saracens' horsemanship and displaying great military skill against the Turkish cavalry of Saladin. In a sense, Richard consolidated the supremacy of the Christian cavalry which El Cid had established over Islam in Spain and he proved this to great effect in the running battles which followed the siege of Acre.

Two knights in quilted armour of the type called gambeson. Though beginning to go out of fashion in Richard's time, many of his soldiers would still have worn it.

The Kingdom of Christ

The siege of Acre began in 1189, when Guy of Lusignan, desperate to renew his failing fortunes, had marched with a suicidally-small force against the greatest city in the Holy Land. Despite lack of strength, his forces had held on grimly; gradually reinforcements had filtered through until they were sufficient to establish a blockade on the landward side of the city.

At that point, a stalemate resulted, with the Christian forces in turn surrounded by Saladin, and enough Saracen ships getting through to keep the besieged forces at Acre sufficiently provisioned. Philip's arrival, shortly before, had considerably boosted the morale of the besiegers. However, Guy of Lusignan was far from pleased since Philip at once began plotting to make himself King of Jerusalem. Added to this, Guy had another adversary in the shape of Conrad of Montferrat, who had won an overwhelming victory against Saladin by repulsing the Moslem attack on Tyre. Thus Conrad's star was in the ascendant, while Guy's fell. It was this situation which had prompted Lusignan to lay siege to Acre and to invite Richard's support.

The arrival of the English King further heartened the attacking force. Not only did Richard bring with him a large army, he also had a number of siege engines with which he began systematically to batter at the walls of Acre.

Richard leads a relief force to the aid of the beleaguered city of Acre. He is the first to leap ashore, to the delight and relief of the garrison commander.

Nevertheless, the state of siege continued for a further month. Both Richard and Philip sickened with what appears to have been a form of scurvy; and for a while Richard's life was threatened. But he was soon well enough to be carried in a litter to within the sight of the battered walls and to offer a gold piece to any man who could bring him a stone from those walls.

The continuing pressure began to tell on the grim defenders of the city. Whenever a section of the walls collapsed – either from the battery of the siege engines or from miners working beneath them – the Christian forces attacked. Upon each attack, the defenders sounded their drums, and Saladin at once attacked the Christian camp from behind.

Nevertheless, the outcome was inevitable and on 12th July 1189, the beleaguered garrison capitulated, agreeing terms of surrender which included a large ransom, the release of 1,500 prisoners held by Saladin, and the restoration of the True Cross, which had been captured during the fall of Jerusalem.

There then occurred one of those events which, though seemingly of minor effect, was to have far-reaching repercussions.

As the triumphant Christian forces entered Acre, the Kings of England and France both set up their standards, thereby claiming not only the victory but also a part of the spoils. Alongside their flags was that of another crusader lord, Duke Leopold of Austria; he had nominal command over the remnant of Emperor Frederick Barbarossa's army, which had continued to Acre after Barbarossa's death. However, despite his honorary title, Leopold had no money to buy his supporters. In contrast, Richard and Philip were trying to outbid each other by offering first three and then four gold pieces to any soldier who took service with them.

This placed Leopold in a very subordinate position, and the act of raising his standard and claiming a share in the booty of the fallen city was a foolish one, to say the least. In fact, his banner flew beside those of England and France for a few hours only. Then it was unceremoniously pulled down and trodden into the mud by English soldiers, who must have been acting with Richard's approval at the very least.

Naturally, Leopold protested, but he was virtually brushed aside. He left the camp a few days later and returned to Austria, but he was not to forget the slight done to him by the English king. Soon, the day was to come when Richard had grave cause to regret his actions and the humiliation of Leopold.

With Acre in the hands of the Christians, Philip now declared his intention of returning to France. Despite every effort of his followers to prevent it, he gave half his share of booty to Conrad of Montferrat. Then, leaving half his army under the command of the Duke of Burgundy, he set sail for home.

Richard was far from happy at this turn of events. He was suspicious of Philip's intentions and extracted a promise from him that the French

During the Siege of Acre, Richard offered a gold piece to any man who would bring him back a stone from the walls of the city.

Richard was a powerful and ruthless adversary, earning his title 'Lionheart' from the Saracens who were his bitterest foes. In a pitched battle, the armour and weaponry of the Christian army proved superior.

King would not attack Angevin lands while he, Richard, remained on the crusade. Then he set about concluding the terms of surrender negotiated with the Moslem garrison of Acre, which involved a large-scale exchange of prisoners. For whatever reason – though possibly a simple one of logistics – Saladin was not able to meet the deadline. Richard therefore had 2,500 prisoners taken outside the walls and executed in sight of Saladin's army. It was an act of barbarism for which there is no reasonable excuse. Richard himself looked on as his soldiers, remembering perhaps their own fallen comrades, fell upon the bound prisoners and literally hacked them to pieces.

Two days later, he marched out of Acre on the next leg of his campaign to win back 'God's Kingdom'. With Philip gone, he was now the senior commander of the crusade. He paid the remnant of the French army from his own coffers in order to prevent them from reducing the

Richard watches coldly as 2,500 Saracen prisoners are executed in front of their comrades after the Battle of Acre.

THE SIEGE OF ACRE 1189-91 and RICHARD'S ROAD TO JERUSALEM 1191-2

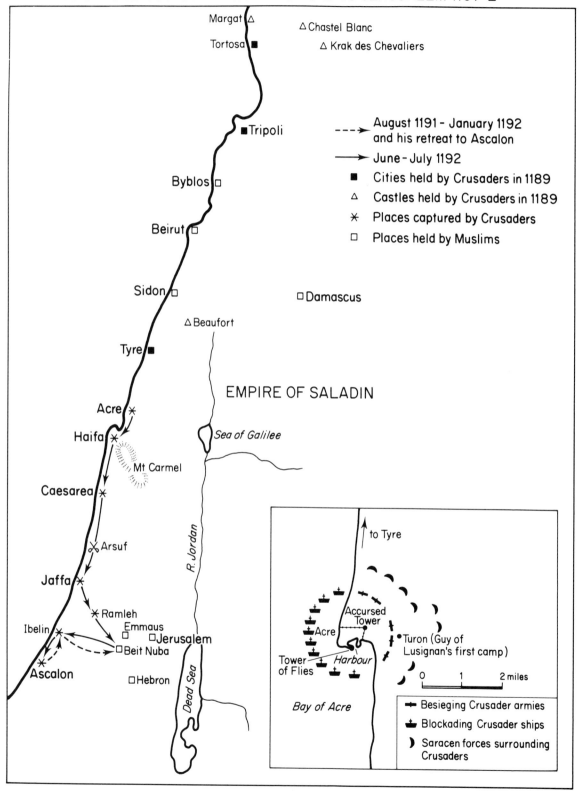

Margat △
Tortosa ■
△ Chastel Blanc
△ Krak des Chevaliers

■ Tripoli

Byblos □

Beirut □

Sidon □
△ Beaufort

Tyre ■

□ Damascus

EMPIRE OF SALADIN

Acre ✳
Haifa ✳
Sea of Galilee
Mt Carmel

Caesarea ✳

R. Jordan

✳ Arsuf

Jaffa ✳

✳ Ramleh
Emmaus
Ibelin ✳
□ □ Jerusalem
✳ □ Beit Nuba
Ascalon ✳
□ Hebron
Dead Sea

- - - → August 1191 – January 1192 and his retreat to Ascalon
——→ June – July 1192
■ Cities held by Crusaders in 1189
△ Castles held by Crusaders in 1189
✳ Places captured by Crusaders
□ Places held by Muslims

Inset map

to Tyre

Accursed Tower
Acre
• Turon (Guy of Lusignan's first camp)
Tower of Flies
Harbour

0   1   2 miles

Bay of Acre

➤ Besieging Crusader armies
⚓ Blockading Crusader ships
) Saracen forces surrounding Crusaders

A crusader sword, typical of the type carried by Richard's army

Christian forces by their departure, and set forth to deal with Saladin.

It has been remarked by more than one historian that, whatever one's bias, the Saracen leader was altogether a more sympathetic character than Richard. Descended from a family of Kurdish army officers, Saladin had become Vizier of Egypt in 1169; and when the ruler of Syria, Nur-el-Din, died in 1174, Saladin married his widow and rapidly established himself as a new champion of the Moslem world. Convinced that it was his destiny to drive the Christians out of the Holy Land, he took up a moral stance as well as a military one. Perhaps because of this, he is remembered as one of the most principled men of his time.

Generous even to his enemies, there is a consistent group of legends which suggest that he made several attempts to seek Richard's friendship. Indeed, there does seem to have existed a grudging respect between the two men who held the reins of power in the Holy Land for the next few years.

Running Battles

Once out of the protection afforded by the walls of Acre, Richard again showed his military genius by the tactics he adopted to deal with Saladin's famous Turkish cavalry.

Richard gave orders that the army should ride in close formation, keeping close to the sea, which thus protected their right flank; the infantry had the task of marching between their left flank and Saladin's force, which kept pace with him and sent in waves of skirmishes to worry him.

This continued all the way to Haifa and beyond. The crusaders suffered terribly from sunstroke, dysentery and the incessant Saracen attack. Yet they kept moving, slowly but surely, provisioned by the fleet which kept pace with them. After several weeks, Saladin at last realized that he must draw Richard into a direct confrontation; only thus would matters be decided.

The Battle of Arsuf took place on 7th October 1195 and lasted for most of the day. Throughout the morning, Richard held in check his strongest force – the mounted knights – and let the infantry take the brunt of the furious Saracen attack. He was waiting for the enemy to be fully engaged and for their mounts to grow tired. Nevertheless, the day was almost lost when the Hospitallers, who had taken a terrible beating, broke and charged. They could have carried the whole Christian army with them and thus opened its ranks to the swiftly weaving attack of the Saracen cavalry. But Richard personally rallied his forces, before they could become demoralized, and lead a tremendous onslaught with all the weight of his knights. They bore all before them. Saladin's hitherto invincible army was cut to ribbons.

A contemporary account says of Richard:

There the King, the fierce, the extraordinary King, cut down the Turks in every direction, and none could escape the force of his army, for wherever he turned, brandishing his sword, he carved a wide path for himself, cutting them down like a reaper with his sickle.

(trans: J. Gillingham.)

Combat between crusaders and Saracens during the period of Richard's activity in the Holy Land.

Three days later, the crusaders reached Jaffa, thus securing the port nearest to Jerusalem. The fleet dropped anchor and began to replenish the exhausted army, while Richard concentrated on constructing temporary walls, Saladin having providently dismantled them before withdrawing some months before.

Indecision and Anticlimax

Richard now had a difficult choice before him. He could advance inland towards Jerusalem, but this would risk his supply lines, which would be thinly stretched between the sea and the army. Alternatively he could continue along the coast to the port of Ascalon, which had greater strategic importance as the base for the Saracen fleet.

For a time, he did neither. Instead, he remained in Jaffa, strengthening its walls and refortifying castles along the road from Acre which Saladin had destroyed. He re-opened negotiations with the Saracen lord, making what now seems the frivolous offer that his sister Joan should marry Saladin's brother and that her dowry should include the coastal towns from Ascalon to Acre. Needless to say, this idea failed to come to anything – though Saladin first of all gave his consent, presumably tongue in cheek, only to be told by Richard that Joan had flatly refused to marry an infidel.

Talks continued throughout the following year. So, too, did the steady, almost secret crusader advance. By December 1191 they were within twelve miles of Jerusalem.

Then, at that point, they turned back. Richard was worried about the increasing pressure on his supply lines. He knew also that even if he succeeded in capturing the Holy City, most of his army would swiftly melt away, their commitment to the crusade satisfied by having set foot on the holy earth at the middle of Christendom.

The whole army was shocked and disheartened by the decision. To many Richard was the greatest general they had known. He had defeated the great Saladin and led them through impossible country to within sight of their goal.

Many wept openly, others cursed their leader; and when the army reached Jaffa, many kept on to Acre, leaving Richard with a much diminished force. Nonetheless, he marched on to Ascalon and took it easily, Saladin having withdrawn to Jerusalem to await an attack which never came.

Richard now controlled the whole of the coastline of Outremer from Acre to Ascalon and swiftly set about consolidating his victories, making the roads safe and rebuilding castles destroyed by the Saracens.

But all was not well in the rest of the country. Political squabbles had broken out again between the supporters of Guy of Lusignan and Conrad of Montferrat. Then, to add to Richard's problems, he received news that his brother John was creating trouble in England, while Philip began threatening the borders of Normandy. It was essential for Richard to return home in order to look after his own affairs. However, before he could do so he had to ensure that Outremer had a strong king – otherwise all that he had achieved would have been lost.

He called a council of crusader lords and asked them to vote for a king. They came down unanimously in favour of Conrad, and Richard had to acknowledge the sense of this: Conrad was the stronger man; Guy had lost the battle of Hattin.

Conrad's triumph was short-lived. A few days later, he was murdered by two of the dreaded order of Assassin, an outlawed Moslem sect who spread a reign of terror throughout the Holy Land.

Conrad's widow, Isabella, had shut herself up in the city of Tyre, acting on her husband's dying instructions not to give up the keys of the city to anyone but Richard. (This was meant to keep it out of French hands.)

Richard's cousin, Henry of Champagne, now appeared on the scene. Incredibly, he wooed and won Isabella and some months later became Lord of Outremer, with Richard's approval. But Henry never styled himself King, since he could not be crowned in Jerusalem.

These events contrived to keep Richard from departing as soon as he had planned. Again, he found himself with two clear choices. He could

return to Europe and put an end to the plotting of John and Philip, but face the possibility of losing all he had gained in Outremer. Equally he could remain in the Holy Land for a longer period and face the possibility of having no lands to which he could return. Added to this dilemma was the pressure from the other crusader lords for him to stay and, under a truly united force, storm Jerusalem at last.

So agonizing was the decision that Richard became ill. When he recovered, he had made up his mind – he would stay until Easter of the following year and he would lead the Christian attack on the Holy City.

Filled with jubilation, the army set forth again to march the long, hot miles back to Jerusalem. Their journey was almost uneventful; but when they once again came within a few miles of their objective, Richard called a halt. Nothing, he realized, had really changed. The same problems as before faced those who succeeded in capturing the city. Suddenly, he declared that he would go no further as leader of the Christian forces. He would accompany them as a pilgrim – or not at all.

Despairing, the army conferred, realized they could never go further without their great captain. Wearily they turned back and marched once again to Ascalon. Once there, Richard re-opened discussions with Saladin, who swiftly agreed to allow the Christian force to remain on the coast, providing they abandoned Ascalon. Richard refused, only to learn that Saladin had marched on Jaffa and laid siege to the Christians within. He turned at once to relieve Jaffa, but arrived to see Saladin's banners already fluttering above the walls.

The garrison were just departing, having laid down their weapons. They saw the relief ships and swiftly renewed the attack. Richard himself leapt into the sea and waded ashore at the head of his men.

Jaffa was soon in crusader hands again. Saladin made a somewhat half-hearted effort at a surprise attack. This was beaten off with resound- ing losses for the Saracens, and Saladin re-opened negotiations for peace.

167

This time, Richard gave in over the question of Ascalon, in return for which the Moslem leader gave pilgrims permission to enter Jerusalem in peace. Richard himself did not avail himself of this offer: he would enter Jerusalem as a conqueror or not at all.

A few weeks later he left the Holy Land. Had he remained until Easter of 1193, as he had originally intended, history might have been very different: Saladin died suddenly in March of that year, thus removing the only real obstacle between the crusaders and the Holy City.

However, Richard was no longer there as leader. His chance of regaining Christ's kingdom had gone forever – and meanwhile an old enemy waited to settle a score.

Capture and Ransom

It had taken Richard far longer to reach the Holy Land than most people of that time. His journey homewards was to be just as protracted and led to an enormous upheaval throughout the Western world.

A few days out from Acre, Richard's fleet was caught in a storm and his ship, the *Franche-Nef*, became separated from the main body of the fleet. Forced to sail on, Richard learned that his enemies were waiting to imprison him at Marseilles. So, after encountering some pirates, whom he first successfully defeated, he then employed them to carry him secretly to a destination on the northern coast of the Adriatic.

However, disaster struck again and the pirate ship was wrecked on lands belonging to the German Emperor Henry VI, who had no cause to love Richard after he had backed Tancred of Sicily against him.

Richard's adventures now assumed an almost legendary quality. He travelled in disguise through the lands of his enemy, was captured, and released again. Finally, he fell into the hands of Duke Leopold of Austria,

who had left the crusades ignominiously after his standard had been torn down by Richard's men and who had borne a grudge ever since.

By now it was the end of 1192; Richard had been 'missing, presumed drowned' for almost a year. All kinds of rumours were rife. In England, Henry Longchamps, who had been left in charge of the kingdom by Richard in his absence, had been virtually overthrown by Prince John who attempted to raise a rebellion with support from disaffected Welsh barons.

It is at this point that there first appears the story of Richard's jongleur, Blondel. Having heard a rumour of his master's capture, Blondel is said to have travelled throughout Europe singing a song he had composed with Richard. He sang until one day he heard a response from a barred window in the castle of Dürnstein.

Whether or not there is any truth in this story, we cannot know. Certainly, there is no hard evidence to support it though it remains one of history's more romantic and well known tales. Whether by this means,

The castle of Dürnstein in Lower Austria where Richard was held to ransom by Archduke Leopold, in retaliation for the insults done to him by Richard's men. Legend has it that Blondel sang beneath the windows and so discovered his imprisoned master.

or by more orthodox communications, it soon became known that Richard was a prisoner, and there at once began a race to see who could raise the largest ransom for him – his friends or his enemies.

Naturally, Philip of France desired to capture his old enemy and lay claim to his lands. Prince John was content to let his brother rot rather than give up the power he had begun to acquire. John had already done homage to Philip for Richard's lands, and had promised to marry Philip's sister Alys, whom Richard had earlier refused.

The ransom for the captive king was set at 20,000 marks, a huge sum by the standard of the time, and various other difficult provisos hedged him round.

Moved from castle to castle to forestall any attempt at rescue, Richard finally faced his enemies at Speyer, not far from Wurtzburg, on 21–22nd March 1193. He was accused of plotting the death of Conrad of Montferrat; of supporting Tancred's illegal regime; and of the insult to Leopold of Austria. So calm, dignified and eloquent was Richard in response, that the Emperor Henry was moved to offer the kiss of peace, while others among his accusers wept openly.

Even so, the ransom was now increased to 100,000 marks, with 70,000 as a downpayment, and a further promise to supply men and arms to the German Emperor for a reconquest of Sicily.

Hard upon the heels of this came news that Philip had openly declared war on the Angevins and had attacked Normandy with some success. In England, John was being kept in check by a few of Richard's loyal supporters, and efforts were under way to raise the huge ransom.

For months, the incessant bargaining continued and Richard was virtually an object for auction among the crowned heads of Europe. Yet he proved himself a better politician than many had supposed, making himself so useful to Henry VI that the two virtually became allies. At one time Richard was even offered the crown of Portugal, which would have extended his empire still further.

Then, fearful of Richard's imminent release, Philip and John jointly made an offer of 150,000 marks in order to buy him from the Germans. This was tempting and would have made Richard a prisoner of Philip. Fortunately, Richard had now made a sufficient number of friends at the German court to ensure that the offer was rejected. However, Henry did raise the ransom money to match the French offer, and also insisted that Richard do homage to him for England.

By this time, the Lionheart was desperate to be free and would probably have agreed to anything. He offered to pay 100,000 marks to Henry and 50,000 to Leopold. So on these terms he was finally set free in March of 1194. He had been a prisoner for two years and his freedom had cost more than three times his own yearly income. He had also lost part of his lands to Philip. But he cared nothing except that he was free.

Leopold of Austria, condemned by the Church for his part in impris-

oning a crusader, refused to pay back the ransom. Strangely, not long after, his foot was crushed by a fall from his horse and he died a few months later from gangrene.

Europe's Champion

Once back in England, Richard set about putting right the wrongs perpetrated by his brother, who had fled to France, and then began finding methods of regaining the money he had lost in buying his release. He intended to cross the channel to Normandy at the first opportunity and win back the lands he had lost to Philip and John.

Ably assisted by his new chancellor, Archbishop Hubert Walter, Richard raised sufficient revenue from the hard-pressed tax-payers of England to raise an army. In May 1194, he entered Normandy to a rapturous welcome. John, suddenly deciding that his brother might win the game they had been playing for the past ten years, left Philip and threw himself on Richard's mercy. Richard forgave him magnanimously, but saw to it that John had no further chance of betrayal.

Richard proceeded to march rings round his old enemy of France, capturing a large amount of booty – and a part of the royal archive which

Richard mortally wounded in the shoulder by an arrow shot by Bertrand de Gourdon, at the siege of Castle Chalus in Limousin, 1199. This depiction is from the fifteenth century manuscript the Chronique de Normandie.

contained the names of those among Richard's supporters who had promised aid to Philip if the need arose.

Richard seemed absolutely unstoppable. He had signed treaties with the Count of Toulouse and the King of Navarre even while he was still in prison. Effectively, he had Philip cut off. Even Pope Innocent III threatened the French King for repudiating the daughter of King Cnut of Denmark, whom he had married in 1193.

But Philip still had a powerful army and had succeeded in capturing a sufficient number of castles along the border of Normandy to enable him to mount raids deep into Richard's territory.

The struggle dragged on into 1195, and despite a treaty signed in January of the following year, hostilities continued, and in 1198 matters had still not improved. Another treaty was finally negotiated in 1199 by a papal legate and the two Kings met briefly, though remaining only in view of each other on separate banks of the Seine. Part of the agreement included a marriage between Philip's son Louis and Richard's niece, Blanche of Castille. It was an agreement which seemed likely to provide a peace both lasting and satisfactory to both sides.

Then disaster struck, and in a few weeks Europe's strongest champion was dead. Richard had always been reckless, allowing himself to be distracted by minor concerns to which others could have attended. Typically, it was this carelessness which cost him his life. Word reached him that a peasant had found some treasure and taken it to his lord, Archard of Chalus, who intended to keep it for himself. Richard thought otherwise, and took a large force to besiege Chalus' small castle. Tradition has it that there were barely fifteen men inside, ill-armed and ill-prepared to withstand a siege. During the fighting Richard received a wound in the shoulder from a cross-bow bolt. The wound festered and the bolt proved difficult to remove. Gangrene entered the wound and Richard realized that he was facing death. He wrote to Eleanor of Aquitaine, incredibly still active at nearly eighty years of age, bequeathing his realm to John, along with three-quarters of his treasure. The rest was to be distributed among the poor.

This sudden act of charity was followed by another generous decision: the man who had wounded him was brought before Richard who forgave him and ordered him set free. Richard then received the last rites and died in the evening, aged forty-one.

The empire he had left behind was no less extensive than that of his father, but it was a great deal less secure. John had none of his family's abilities and is typically remembered by the nickname 'Lackland'. Only a few years after he became king, he was forced to sign Magna Carta, giving more power than ever before to the barons of the realm. The loss of the royal treasure in the Wash concluded a catalogue of disasters. Perhaps in the shadow of a legend, he could have done no better.

Lionheart – Legend and Legacy

Richard *Coeur de Lion*, the Lionheart of England, was dead. He had already become something of a legend, and despite all his shortcomings,

This portrait of Richard I is based on contemporary pictures. He was short, red-haired and of a fiery, sometimes, ill-natured, sometimes generous temper.

it is in this light that he is remembered. Yet he failed in his greatest enterprise: the capture of the Holy City. Equally, he was a poor king and a hotheaded – if courageous – leader, who died carelessly and without leaving an heir to his great empire.

When Archbishop Walter visited Jerusalem in 1192, he met Saladin and the two men discussed Richard at length. The Saracen who had been Richard's greatest enemy, had this to say:

> I have long since been aware that your king is a man of honour and very brave, but he is impudent, indeed absurdly so, in the way he plunges into the midst of danger and in his reckless indifference to his own safety . . . I would like to have wisdom and moderation rather than an excessive wildness.

(trans: J. Gillingham)

His words proved fatally apt, but the legend only continued to grow after Richard's death. He had first received the title Lionheart at the start of the Crusade, when someone compared Philip to a lamb and Richard to a lion, and seemed to become beset with mythical associations. He is said to have convened his commanders in Winchester at the Round Table, believed to have belonged to King Arthur, and to have possessed the magical sword Excalibur. Later legends and popular folklore describe his meeting with Robin Hood in Sherwood Forest, and commend him for his resistance to John Lackland's plots. Indeed, it is this almost Hollywood-like story which is most familiar to us.

Saladin receiving the Bishop of Salisbury and other Christian pilgrims, whom he treated with respect and eventually permitted to enter Jerusalem.

The statue of Richard which
stands outside of the Houses of
Parliament in London.

At his death, the troubador, Gaucelem Faidit mourned him as 'the
courageous and powerful King of the English,' and men who had fought
at his side praised his courage and leadership.

As John Gillingham, one of his most recent biographers observed, it is
a mistake to judge Richard by modern standards. As a man of the twelfth
century, he was neither better nor worse than many others. As a symbol
of the burgeoning chivalric ideals of the time, he was bound to be
enshrined as a hero of his age. It is best that as such we remember him,
forgetting the darker side of his nature – the slaughter of 2,500 prisoners
at Acre and the greed which undoubtedly motivated much of his life.
Better indeed, to remember him as a warrior in the heroic mould; a man
who, in the end, would not have disappointed his exacting father.

He was Europe's Lionheart, and as such he continues to inspire with
an idea of nobility which he may never have known. As well as a
warrior, he was also a poet and a troubador who wrote a number of
songs which have survived. One of these, written while he was still in

prison, sums him up best and perhaps serves best as a reminder of his finer qualities:

Ja nus hons pris ne dira sa raison
adroitement, se dolantement non;
mes par confort puet il fere chançon.
moult ai amis, mes povre sont li don;
honte en avront, se por mes reançon
sui ces deus yvers pris.

Ce servent bien mi homme et mi baron,
Englois, Normant, Poitevin et Gascon,
que je n'avoir si povre conpaignon,
cui je laissasse por avoir en prixon.
je nel di pas por nule retraçon,
mes encor sui ge pris.

No prisoner pleads well his case,
Framing it sorrowfully. But,
To comfort his distress, he can make a song.
My friends are many, though their gifts are few.
Shame upon them, if my ransom is not paid
These two winters in prison.

My friends and barons know well -
English, Norman, Poitevin and Gascon all -
That no friend of mine so low
Would I leave in prison for want of cash.
I mean no reproach
But still am I held captive.
        (*Richard Coeur de Lion* trans: Caitlín Matthews)

The Romance of Richard Coeur de Lion

The following three extracts are from a redaction of a fourteenth century English romance based on an earlier French work. It contains a strange mixture of history and fantastic invention: the account of the Crusade being more or less accurate, but with the addition of episodes of imaginary adventures demonstrating the way in which Richard had become a larger-than-life figure of truly mythic proportions. They tell the curious story of Richard's birth, and of his single combat with Saladin. They are taken from George Ellis' *Specimens of Early English Metrical Romances* of 1848, further edited by the present author. They give a startling portrait of Richard, very far from that of history, but very much in the manner of the time and of the legendary quality possessed by the King.

The Birth of a Hero
Lord, King of Glory, what favours didst thou bestow on King Richard! How edifying is it to read the history of his conquests! Many acts of

Some of Richard's soldiers are aggrieved by the proud claims of the Austrian Archduke Leopold, who raised his standard between those of England and France. They pull down the Austrian standard, trampling it in the mud.

chivalry are familiarly known; the deeds of Charlemagne and Turpin, and of their knights Ogier le Danois, Roland, and Oliver; those of Alexander; those of Arthur and Gawain; and even the ancient wars of Troy and the exploits of Hector and Achilles, are already current in rhyme. But the glory of Richard and of the peerless knights of England, his companions, is at present exhibited only in French books, which not more than one in a hundred of unlearned men can understand. This story, lordings, I propose to tell you; and may the blessing of God be on those who will listen to me with attention!

The father of Richard was King Henry; in whose reign, as I find in my original, Saint Thomas was slain at the altar of the cathedral of Canterbury, where miracles are wrought to this day. King Henry, when twenty years of age, was a prince of great valour; but having a dislike to matrimony, could not be induced to take a wife on account of her wealth or power; and only acceded to the entreaties of his barons, on the condition of their providing for his consort the most beautiful woman in the universe.

Ambassadors were immediately dispatched in every direction to search for this paragon. One party of them was carried, by a fair wind, into the midst of the ocean, where they were suddenly arrested by a calm which threatened to prevent the further prosecution of their voyage. Fortunately, the breeze had already brought them nearly in contact with another vessel, which by its astonishing magnificence engrossed their whole attention. Every nail seemed to be headed with gold; the deck was painted with azure and inlaid with ivory; the rudder appeared to be of pure gold; the mast was of ivory; the sails of satin; the ropes of silk; an awning of cloth of gold was spread above the deck; and under this awning were assembled divers knights and ladies most superbly dressed, appearing to form the court of a princess whose beauty was bright as the sun through the glass. Our ambassadors were hailed by this splendid company, and questioned about the object of their voyage: which being explained, they were conducted on board, and received with proper ceremony by the stranger king, who rose from his chair, composed of a single carbuncle stone, to salute them. Trestles were immediately set; a table covered with a silken cloth was laid; a rich repast, ushered in by the sound of trumpets and shalms, was served up; and the English knights had full leisure during dinner to contemplate the charms of the incomparable princess, who was seated near her father. The king then informed them that he had been instructed by a vision to set sail for England with his daughter; and the ambassadors, delighted at finding the success of their search confirmed with this preternatural authority, proposed to accompany him without loss of time to their master. A north-easterly wind springing up at the moment, they set sail, entered the Thames, and soon cast anchor off the Tower; where King Henry happened to be lodged, and was informed by his ambassadors of their safe arrival.

A Knight Templar, the most feared order of knighthood in the Holy Land. They were monks as well as warriors, dedicated to a spiritual life and to the recapture of the holy places in Jerusalem. They guided and protected pilgrims during the Middle Ages.

Returning home to England in disguise, Richard was recognized and attacked by soldiers of Archduke Leopold of Austria, who subsequently kept the Lionheart hostage.

Henry made immediate preparations for the reception of the royal visitors. Attended by his whole court, he went to meet and welcome them at the water-side; from whence the whole company, preceded by bands of minstrels, marched in procession to the royal palace at Westminster, the streets through which they passed being hung with cloth of gold. A magnificent entertainment was provided; after which Henry having thus fulfilled the duties of hospitality addressed the stranger king:

> 'Lief Sire, what is thy name?'
> 'My name,' he said, 'is Corbaring;
> Of Antioch I am king.'
> And told him, in his resoun [oration],
> He came thither thorough a vision.
> 'For sothe, Sire, I telle thee,
> I had else brought more meynie;
> Many mo, withouten fail,
> And mo shippes with vitail.'
> Then asked he that lady bright,
> 'What hightest thou, my sweet wight?'
> 'Cassodorien, withouten leasing.'
> Thus answered she the king.
> 'Damsel,' he said, 'bright and sheen,
> Wilt thou dwell and be my queen?'
> She answered, with words still,
> 'Sire, I am at my father's will.'

After this courtship the king of Antioch, who was no friend to unnecessary delays, proposed that they should be betrothed on that night; and that the nuptials, which he wished to be private, should be celebrated on the following morning.

These conditions were readily accepted, and the fair Cassodorien received the nuptial benediction; but the ceremony was attended with an untoward accident. At the elevation of the host, the young queen fainted away; and her swoon continued so long that it became necessary to carry her out of church into an adjoining chamber. The spectators were much alarmed at this unlucky omen; and she was herself so disturbed by it, that she made a vow never more to assist at any of the sacraments: but it does not seem to have much interrupted the happiness of the royal couple, because the queen became successively the mother of three children; Richard, John, and a daughter named Topyas.

During fifteen years, Cassodorien was permitted to persevere in her resolution without any remonstrance from King Henry; but unluckily, after this period, one of his principal barons remarked to him that her conduct gave general scandal, and requested his permission to detain her in church from the commencement of the mass till its termination. Henry consented; and when the queen, on hearing the bell which announced the celebration of the sacrament, prepared to leave the church, the baron opposed her departure, and attempted to detain her by force. The event of the experiment was extraordinary. Cassodorien,

seizing her daughter with one hand, and Prince John with the other,

A battle at sea between crusaders and Saracens. On his way to the Holy Land, Richard met with one of the ships running the blockade around Acre. He defeated the Moslem sailors with consummate ease.

> *Out of the roof she gan her dight* [prepared to depart]
> *Openly, before all their sight!*
> *John fell from the air, in that stound,*
> *And brake his thigh on the ground;*
> *And with her daughter she fled away,*
> *That never after she was y-seye* [seen].

Henry repented, when it was too late, of his deference to the advice of his courtiers. Inconsolable for the loss of the beautiful Cassodorien, he languished for a short time, and then died, leaving his dominions to his eldest son Richard, who was now in his fifteenth year, and was already distinguished by his premature excellence in all the exercises of chivalry.

Battle at Sea
Richard now prepared for his grand expedition, and, having confided

the government of Cyprus to the Earl of Leicester, set sail for Syria with a fleet of two hundred transports under convoy of fifteen well-armed galleys. For the first ten days the weather was perfectly favourable; but on the eleventh they met with a violent storm, during which it was difficult to prevent the dispersion of the armament. At length the sky cleared, and they discovered in the offing a *dromound,* or ship of burthen of vast size, and laden nearly to the water's edge. Alain Trenchemer was dispatched, in a light vessel, to inquire whither she was bound, whose property she was, and what was her cargo and was answered by a *latimer* (an interpreter) that she came from Apulia, was laden with provisions for the use of the French army, and was bound to Acres. But Alain, perceiving only one man on deck who answered his questions, insisted on seeing the rest of the crew, whom he suspected to be Saracens; and after a few evasions on the part of the latimer, the whole ship's company suddenly came upon deck, and answered him by a general shout of defiance. Alain hastily returned with this report to the king; who, arming himself with all expedition, threw himself into a galley, and ordered his rowers to make every possible exertion.

> 'Roweth on fast! Who that is faint,
> In evil water may he be dreynt!'
> They rowed hard, and sung thereto
> With hevelow and rumbeloo.

Richard's impatience being thus seconded by the zeal of his men, the galley flew like an arrow from a cross-bow; and Alain steered the vessel with such skill, that, encountering the stern of the dromound, it cut off a considerable part of her quarter. The king made every effort to board; but the deck was covered with well-armed Saracens; and others from the 'top castles' assaulted the galley with such showers of heavy stones, that Richard was in the most imminent danger. At length, seven more galleys being detached to his assistance, and the enemies attacked in every direction, he sprang on board of the dromound, and, setting his back against the mast, clove many of the Saracens to the middle, cut off the heads of others, and amputated arms and legs in every direction; till the unbelievers, who at first consisted of sixteen hundred men, were reduced to thirty.

A Fatal Combat

It was now determined to attempt, without further delay, the siege of Nineveh; but intelligence being received that the Saracens were assembling in great numbers in the plain of Odoh, it became necessary to defeat them in the first instance. Richard, dividing the Christians into four parts, directed them to take different routes, so as to arrive on the field and make their attack on four opposite points: he also ordered them to display only the Saracen standards which they had captured in the field of Arsour. By this stratagem the enemy were completely surprised and routed, excepting a small body, which, not being pressed with sufficient vigour by Philip's division, retreated in good order to Nineveh.

The siege of that city was next undertaken; and the military engines being brought up to the walls, the mangonels began to cast stones, and at the same time

Arrowblast of vys, with quarrell,
With staff-slings that smite well,
With trepegettes they slungen also;
That wrought hem full mickle wo!
And blew wild fire in trumpes of gin
To mickle sorrow to hem within.

But these tardy operations were soon suspended by a proposal from the garrison, to which King Richard most joyfully consented; viz., that the fate of the place and of its dependencies should be decided by a combat between three Saracen and three Christian champions. Sir Archolyn, Sir Coudyrbras, and Sir Calabre were respectively opposed to Richard, Sir Thomas Tourneham, and Sir Fulk Doyley, and had the honour of contesting, for a short time, the victory with the three bravest knights in the world. The issue of the combat, however, proved fatal to the Mahometan champions; the city was surrendered; and the garrison and inhabitants, who had been spectators of the battle, being convinced that the best religion was that which conferred military superiority, came in crowds to be baptized, and to follow the standard of the conquerors.

Saladin, in the mean time, had retreated to Babylon, where he again assembled a vast army; but, being surprised by the sudden march of his enemies, was unexpectedly besieged by them in his capital. The Christians, well aware of the advantage of attacking him in a position where his cavalry was perfectly useless, lost no time in completing the blockade.

Richard, always indefatigable, harassed the besieged by constant night attacks, in which the flights of quarrells and arrows from his engines did great execution; and, during the day, employed his mangonels to beat down the outworks and approaches to the city. In short, the romancer assures us that the destruction of Saladin and his whole army would have been unavoidable, had not Philip been bribed by the vast treasures sent by the besieged to withdraw his forces, under pretence of wanting provisions, and thus to prevent the continuation of the blockade.

Saladin, being thus enabled to meet his enemy once more in the field, sent a messenger to offer battle; and at the same time a challenge to King Richard, to meet him in single combat in front of the two armies, for the purpose of deciding their respective pretensions, and of ascertaining whether 'Jesus or Jupiter' was the more powerful divinity. The challenge was accompanied by the offer of a war-horse, far superior in strength and activity to Favel of Cyprus or Lyard of Prys (the favourite horses of Richard), which it was proposed that he should ride on the occasion.

It seems that a necromancer, a 'noble clerk', had conjured two 'strong

A Knight Hospitaller. Together with the Templars, they were the greatest and most feared soldiers in the Holy Land.

181

fiends of the air' into the likeness of a mare and her colt; and that the younger devil had received instructions to kneel down and suck his dam as often as she, by neighing, should give him a signal for the purpose. Such an attitude could not but prove very inconvenient to his rider, who would thus be nearly at the mercy of his antagonist; and it was hoped that Saladin, being mounted on the mare, would obtain an easy victory. Richard, ignorant of this conspiracy against his life and honour, readily accepted all the conditions; the horse was sent on the morning of the battle to the Christian camp; and the hopes of the fiend and of the Sultan seemed on the point of being realized.

But, during the preceding night, an angel had appeared to the Christian hero; had related the machinations of the Saracens; had given him full instructions for the management of his diabolical steed; and had presented to him a spearhead, which no armour, however enchanted, was able to resist. At the first dawn of day the hostile armies began to form in order of battle. That of the Saracens, occupying an extent of ten miles in front, threatened to surround the inferior forces of the Christians;

> As snow ligges on the mountains,
> Be-helied [covered over] were hills and plains,
> With hauberk bright and helmes clear.
> Of trumpes and of tabourer
> To hear the noise it was wonder:
> As though the earth above and under
> Should fallen, so fared the sound!

Richard, however, perfectly indifferent about the numbers of the infidels, pointed them out to his troops as a multitude of victims whom heaven had destined to sacrifice; and, calling for his arms and horse, immediately prepared for battle.

The fiend horse being led forth, the king, in conformity to the angel's instructions, conjured him, in the name of the Trinity, to submit to his guidance in the battle; and the fiend having shaken his head in token of acquiescence, he ordered that the creature's ears should be closely stopped with wax, and that he should be caparisoned in the manner prescribed by the messenger of Heaven.

The reins of his bridle, the crupper, the girths, and the peytrel [*breast plate*] were of steel chain; the saddle-bows were of iron, and supported two hooks, by which was fixed a ponderous beam of wood, forty feet in length, lying across the horse's mane, and intended to bear down, at every evolution of the animal, whatever body of enemies might attempt to oppose his progress. From the lower part of the saddle-bows were suspended on one side the formidable battle-axe, always so fatal to the Saracens, and on the other a brazen club. The king, arrayed in splints of steel, which were again covered by a complete coat of mail; his helmet surmounted by the dove perching on a cross, the symbol of the Holy Ghost; his shield, emblazoned with three leopards, on his shoulder; and bearing in his hand the spear, on whose point was engraven the holy name of God, only waited till the terms of the battle between himself and Saladin should be publicly read, and assented to by both parties; and then, springing into the saddle, set spurs to his steed, and flew with the rapidity of lightning to the encounter.

Saladin, throwing his shield before him, rushed to the charge with equal impetuosity; but as he trusted principally to his mare, he was unwilling to encumber himself with a spear, and only bore in his hand a broad scymitar, with which he proposed to cut off the head of his prostrate enemy. The mare, indeed, exerted herself to the utmost: she shook with violence the numberless bells with which her bridle and housings were completely covered, and neighed with all her might; but the colt-fiend, whose ears were closely stopped, was insensible to a noise, which almost deafened both armies. Far from relaxing, he seemed to increase his speed, and met his unfortunate dam with a shock which she was not all prepared to resist.

Her girth and bridle instantly burst; she rolled on the plain: at the same time the spear of Richard passed through the serpent painted on the sultan's shield, penetrated his armour and part of the shoulder, and threw him, with his heels in the air, to a distance on the plain. Richard, without further troubling himself about the sultan or his mare, rode at full speed into the midst of the Saracen phalanx; overset with his beam twenty unbelievers on each side of his saddle; and, whirling his battle-axe, beheaded or clove to the chine every enemy within his reach. The earl of Salisbury, Doyley, Tourneham, and his other brave knights closely followed, and assisted in dissipating such of the enemy as ventured to resist; and Philip, with his Frenchmen, valiantly assailed the fugitives.

The rout soon became general:

> To tell the sooth in all things,
> In the Gest as we find,
> That mo than sixty thousand
> Of empty steeds abouten yode
> Up to the fetlocks in blood.

In the mean time, the citizens of Babylon, seeing from their walls the defeat of their countrymen, opened their gates to the victors; and Saladin, when recovered from his fall, seeing that all was lost, set spurs to his mare, and escaped into a thick wood, where Richard, encumbered by his beam, was unable to follow him.

Of the inhabitants of Babylon, the greater number consented to be baptized: those who refused were, as usual, put to the sword; and the riches found in the town were distributed among the conquerors, who, after a fortnight spent in feasts and rejoicing, proceeded on their march towards Jerusalem, the reduction of which seemed to promise no considerable difficulty.

★ ★ ★

Tho afterward, all the three year,
Christian men, both far and near,
Yeden the way to Jerusalem,
To the sepulchre, and to Bethlem,
To Olivet, and to Nazarel,
And to Imaus castel,
And to all other pilgrimage,
Withouten harm or damage.
King Richard, doughty of hand,
Turned homeward to England.
King Richard reigned here
No more but ten year.
Sithen, he was shot, alas!
In castel Gaillard there he was.
Thus ended Richard our King:
God give us all good ending!
And his soul rest and roo [repose],
And our souls, when we come thereto!
  Amen. Explicit.

The Abbey of Fontrevault in the Loire valley, founded in the twelfth century by Benedictine nuns, became the burial place of many of the Plantagenets. The magnificent tombs contain the remains of Henry II, Eleanor of Aquitaine, Isabella of Angouleme (wife of John) and the Lionheart himself, whose tomb effigy is shown here.

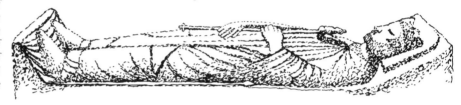

GENEALOGY OF CHARACTERS

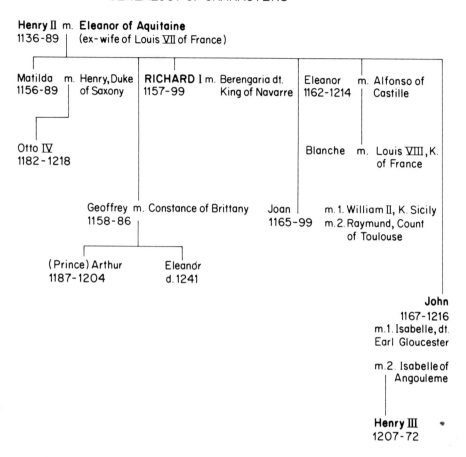

Henry II m. **Eleanor of Aquitaine**
1136-89 │ (ex-wife of Louis VII of France)

Matilda m. Henry, Duke
1156-89 of Saxony

RICHARD I m. Berengaria dt.
1157-99 King of Navarre

Eleanor m. Alfonso of
1162-1214 Castille

Otto IV
1182-1218

Blanche m. Louis VIII, K.
of France

Geoffrey m. Constance of Brittany
1158-86

Joan
1165-99

m.1. William II, K. Sicily
m.2. Raymund, Count
of Toulouse

(Prince) Arthur
1187-1204

Eleanor
d. 1241

John
1167-1216
m.1. Isabelle, dt.
Earl Gloucester

m.2. Isabelle of
Angouleme

Henry III
1207-72

Bibliography

Barber, R. *The Devil's Crown* BBC, 1978
Barber, R. *The Reign of Chivalry* David and Charles, 1980
Billings, M. *The Cross and the Crescent* BBC, 1987.
Bridge, A. *The Crusades* Granada, 1980
Duggan, A. *The Devil's Brood* Faber & Faber, 1957
Foss, M. *Chivalry* Book Club Associates, 1975
Fossier, R. (ed.) *Cambridge Illustrated History of the Middle Ages 1250–1520* Cambridge University Press, 1986
Gillingham, J. *The Life & Times of Richard I* Weidenfeld & Nicolson, 1973
Hallam, E. (ed.) *The Plantagenet Chronicles* Weidenfeld & Nicolson, 1986
Hampden, J. (ed.) *Crusader King* Ward, 1956
Henderson, P. *Richard Coeur de Lion* Hale, 1958

Holbach, M.M. *In the Footsteps of Richard Coeur de Lion* Stanley Paul, 1912
Keen, M. *Chivalry* Yale University Press, 1984
Koch, H.W. *Medieval Warfare* Bison Books, 1978
Koenigsburger, H.G. *Medieval Europe* Longmans, 1987
Newark, T. *Medieval Warfare* Jupiter Books, 1979
Newark, T. *Medieval Warlords* Blandford Press, 1987
Norgate, K. *Richard the Lion Heart* Longman, 1924
Runicman, S. *A History of the Crusades* Cambridge University Press, 1951-4
Tarassuk, L. and Blair, C. (ed.) *The Complete Encyclopedia of Arms and Weapons* Batsford, 1979
Turnbull, S. *The World of the Medieval Knight* Arms & Armour Press, 1986

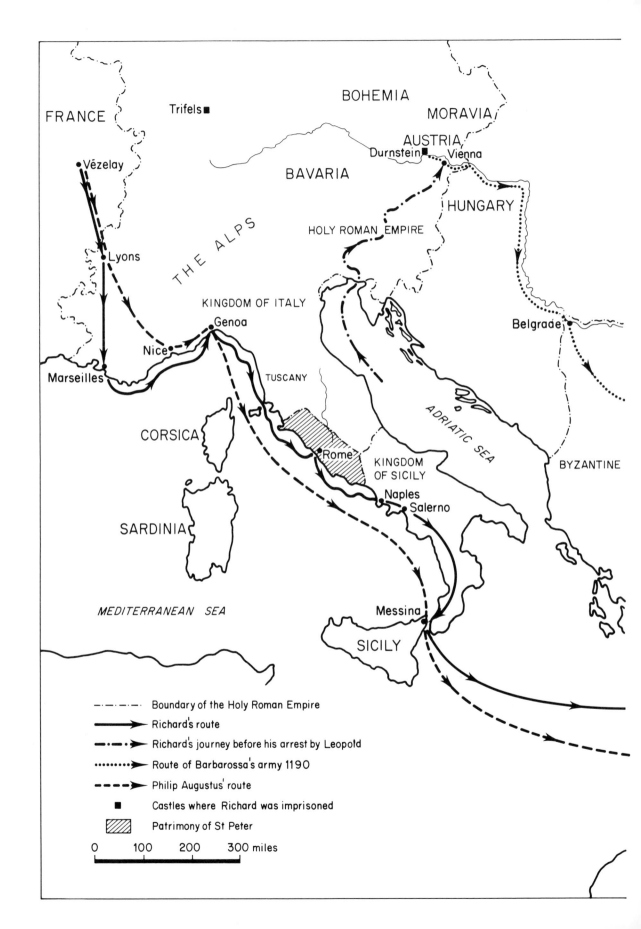

BOHEMIA

MORAVIA

AUSTRIA

FRANCE

Trifels■

BAVARIA

Durnstein■ Vienna

HUNGARY

Vézelay

THE ALPS

HOLY ROMAN EMPIRE

Lyons

KINGDOM OF ITALY

Belgrade

Genoa

Nice

TUSCANY

Marseilles

CORSICA

ADRIATIC SEA

Rome

KINGDOM
OF SICILY

Naples
Salerno

SARDINIA

BYZANTINE

MEDITERRANEAN SEA

Messina

SICILY

- - - - - Boundary of the Holy Roman Empire

————▶ Richard's route

—·—·—▶ Richard's journey before his arrest by Leopold

········▶ Route of Barbarossa's army 1190

— — —▶ Philip Augustus' route

■ Castles where Richard was imprisoned

▨ Patrimony of St Peter

0   100   200   300 miles

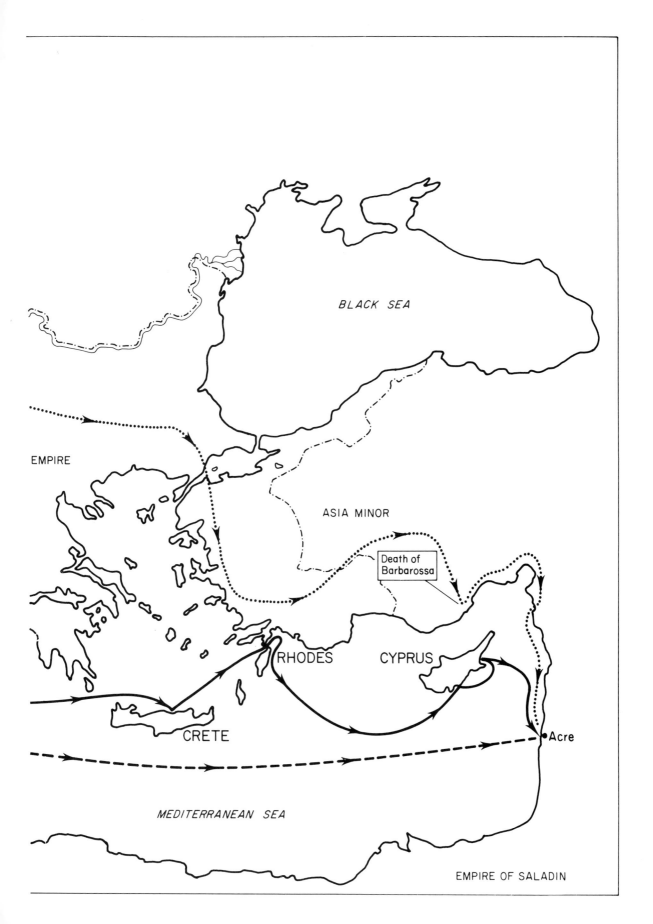

BLACK SEA

EMPIRE

ASIA MINOR

Death of
Barbarossa

RHODES

CYPRUS

CRETE

Acre

MEDITERRANEAN SEA

EMPIRE OF SALADIN

Index

Page numbers in *italics* refer to illustrations.

Illustrations

Colour plates by James Field

Line illustrations by Chesca Potter

Maps and diagrams by Chartwell Illustrators

Photographs and other illustrations courtesy of: Bilothek des Rijksuniversiteit Leiden/Weidenfeld & Nicolson Archive (page 21); Bildarchiv Foto Marburg (pages 101, 117, 119, 123, 125, 127, 128, 130, 131, 134, 135, 159 and 169); Bildarchiv Foto Marburg/Weidenfeld & Nicolson Archive (pages 37 and 45); Cyprus Tourist Board (page 157); Department of the Environment Crown Copyright (page 175); French Government Tourist Office (pages 171 and 184); Mediatheque Municipale Cambrai/ Weidenfeld & Nicoloson Archive (page 23); Peter Newark's Historical Pictures (pages 6, 10, 11, 14, 27, 36, 41, 46, 47, 48, 61, 75, 85, 129, 151, 155, 162, 165, 172, 173, 174 and 179); Spanish National Tourist Board (pages 54, 59, 64, 73, 77 and 83); Stadtsbildstelle Aachen/Weidenfeld & Nicolson Archive (page 8); Stiftsbibliothek St Gallen/Weidenfeld & Nicolson Archive (pages 17 and 25)